CONTENTS

Studies in the Modern Russian Language

GENERAL EDITOR: DENNIS WARD
Professor of Russian, University of Edinburgh

4

EXPRESSION OF
THE PASSIVE VOICE

W. HARRISON
Lecturer in Russian, University of Durham

5

AGREEMENT OF
THE VERB-PREDICATE WITH
A COLLECTIVE SUBJECT

J. MULLEN
Lecturer in Russian, University of Birmingham

CAMBRIDGE
AT THE UNIVERSITY PRESS
1967

CAMBRIDGE UNIVERSITY PRESS
Cambridge, New York, Melbourne, Madrid, Cape Town, Singapore,
São Paulo, Delhi, Dubai, Tokyo, Mexico City

Cambridge University Press
The Edinburgh Building, Cambridge CB2 8RU, UK

Published in the United States of America by Cambridge University Press, New York

www.cambridge.org
Information on this title: www.cambridge.org/9780521094610

First published 1967
Re-issued 2010

A catalogue record for this publication is available from the British Library

Library of Congress Catalogue Card Number: 67–18314

ISBN 978-0-521-09461-0 Paperback

EXPRESSION OF THE PASSIVE VOICE

by W. HARRISON

1. INTRODUCTORY

When confronted by a passive construction which he has to translate into Russian, the English-speaking student is often perplexed by the variety of Russian constructions which appear to be open to him. He will have been told that the imperfective passive is rendered by a reflexive verb: Дом стро́ился (the house was being built), but he will probably realize that he cannot say Он люби́лся for 'he was loved', and that he must use an imperfective passive participle—Он был люби́м. So he may wonder whether to use an imperfective reflexive verb or an imperfective passive participle. Or he may need an imperfective passive participle of a verb which in fact has no such participle: 'the window *being washed* by the workman'. Can he use the reflexive participle мо́ющееся since мы́ться has no present passive participle? When could the reflexive participle be ambiguous, having a reflexive, not a passive meaning? And if the sentence to be translated is 'The sky was covered by clouds' should he use a past passive participle—не́бо бы́ло покры́то облака́ми—or would the reflexive perfective verb be preferable—не́бо покры́лось облака́ми? Or would it not be better to turn the sentence round and make it active anyway? These are some of the problems which this article will try to elucidate.

2. EXPRESSION OF PASSIVE VOICE—GENERAL OUTLINE

From these introductory remarks it will be seen that there are three main means of expressing the passive voice in Russian:

(1) *Reflexive verbs*, normally, but not always, in the imperfective aspect:

Imperfective:

Из хрусталя́ и цеме́нта стро́ились ба́нки, мю́зик-хо́ллы... (A. N. Tolstoy, Хожде́ние по му́кам)	From glass and cement were built banks, music-halls...

5

Perfective:

Це́лый го́род вы́строился здесь за одну́ ночь...
(Leonov, Доро́га на океа́н)

A whole city was built here in one night.

Reflexive participles are, of course, also used with passive meaning:

Дом, строя́щийся на на́шей у́лице...

The house being built in our street...

(2) *Passive participles*, which are usually in the short form when used with быть to form a passive conjugation.

There are three passive participles in Russian:

(*a*) an imperfective participle formed from the present tense and thus called the present passive participle; such as чита́емый, люби́мый.

Все они́ люби́ли кого́-то и бы́ли люби́мы.   (Trofimov, Студе́нты)

They all loved somebody and were loved.

Ива́н Ильи́ч попа́л в спи́сок лиц, подозрева́емых в сочу́вствии рабо́чим.
(A. N. Tolstoy, Хожде́ние по му́кам)

Ivan Il'ich got into the list of persons suspected of sympathy with the workers.

(*b*) an imperfective participle formed from the past tense and called the imperfective past passive participle, such as чи́танный, слы́шанный, би́тый, ви́денный, пи́санный.

Когда́ поверну́л бревно́ — запи́ска...Пи́сана черни́льным карандашо́м.   (Fedin, Города́ и го́ды)

When he turned over the log—a note. ...It was written with an indelible pencil...

(*c*) a perfective past passive participle, such as прочи́танный, услы́шанный, разби́тый, напи́санный.

Статья́ была́ напи́сана по-ру́сски.
(Leonov, Доро́га на океа́н)

The article was written in Russian.

(3) *Conversion to an active construction.* The following examples are active constructions in Russian, whereas the idea would probably be expressed by a passive in English:

Пусть зна́ют лю́ди, за что сня́ли профе́ссора. (Trofimov, Студе́нты)

Let people know why the professor has been removed.

Меня́ развесели́ла найвность, с како́й вы зева́ли на балага́ны.
(Fedin, Города́ и го́ды)

I was amused by the naivety with which you were gaping at the booths.

These methods of expressing the passive voice are discussed in detail in the following sections.

3. EXPRESSION OF THE PASSIVE VOICE BY REFLEXIVE VERBS

A. *The scope of the use of reflexive verbs in expressing the imperfective passive*

Reflexive verbs form the chief means of expressing the passive in the Imperfective aspect.

The verb may be in the *present* tense:

И он, Вадим Бе́лов, кото́рый лу́чше други́х внал, что́ де́лается в стране́, что́ восстано́влено, что́ стро́ится, где поднима́ются но́вые города́...что сде́лал он за два с полови́ной года?
(Trofimov, Студе́нты)

And he, Vadim Belov, who knew better than anyone else what was being done in the country, what had been restored, what was being built where new cities were rising...What had he achieved in two and a half years?

Лиши́в в 22 поколе́ниях 1595 мыше́й хвосто́в, он доказа́л, что приобретённые механи́ческие повреждёния по насле́дству не передаю́тся. (Огонёк)

By depriving 1595 mice in 22 generations of their tails, he proved that acquired mechanical injuries are not transmitted by heredity.

Or the verb may be *future*:

Внизу́, на пе́рвом этаже́, вы́ставка образцо́в, кото́рые сего́дня бу́дут обсужда́ться. (Огонёк)

Below, on the ground floor, is an exhibition of the models which will be discussed today.

Or the verb may be in the *past* tense:

В после́днее десятиле́тие с невероя́тной быстрото́й создава́лись грандио́зные предприя́тия...Из хрусталя́ и цеме́нта стро́ились ба́нки, мюзик-хо́ллы, ске́тинги, великоле́пные кабаки́, где лю́ди оглуша́лись му́зыкой, отраже́нием зерка́л, полуобнажённными же́нщинами, све́том, шампа́нским... В го́роде была́ эпиде́мия самоуби́йств. За́лы суда́ наполня́лись то́лпами истери́ческих же́нщин, жа́дно внима́ющих крова́вым и возбужда́ющим проце́ссам.
(A. N. Tolstoy, Хожде́ние по му́кам)

In the last decade grandiose enterprises had been created...From glass and cement had been built banks, music-halls, skating-rinks, magnificent saloons where people were stupefied by the music, the reflections in the mirrors, half-naked women, light, champagne...There was an epidemic of suicides in the city. The courtrooms were filled with hysterical women listening to bloody and exciting cases.

The verb may be an *infinitive*:

А всё-таки доро́га продолжа́ла стро́иться.
(Leonov, Доро́га на океа́н)

Nevertheless the road went on being built.

7

Сказу́емое мо́жет выража́ться имени́тельным падежо́м и́мени существи́тельного.

(Lomtev, Осно́вы си́нтаксиса...)

The predicate may be expressed by the nominative case of a noun.

По мне́нию э́тих лингви́стов, умозаключе́ния о фа́ктах языка́ должны́ де́латься на основа́нии непосре́дственного наблюде́ния за отде́льным конкре́тным конте́кстом.
Ibid.

In the opinion of these linguists conclusions about the facts of language should be made on the basis of the direct examination of an individual concrete context.

The verb may be in the form of a gerund, though this usage is rare:

Но они́ запада́ли в па́мять и, до́лго не забыва́ясь, та́йно волнова́ли пото́м.   (Trofimov, Студе́нты)

But they were imprinted on his memory, and, since they were remembered for a long time, secretly disturbed him later.

It has already been pointed out that reflexive participles may be used to express the passive:[1]

Взгляну́в на сни́мок, вы, наве́рное, поду́маете, что э́то стро́ящийся кора́бль.   (Огонёк)

Looking at the photograph, you will probably think that this is a ship being built.

The subject may be *animate*:

Строи́тели хорошо́ опла́чиваются.
(Abramov, Вокру́г да о́коло)

The builders are well paid.

Шло обсужде́ние пригово́ра; вне зави́симости от реше́ния по де́лу самого́ Сайфу́ллы, Решёткин выводи́лся из соста́ва бюро́ и назнача́лся в слесаря́; Скуря́тников получа́л оконча́тельное увольне́ние.   (Leonov, Доро́га на океа́н)

Discussion of the verdict was in progress; independently of the decision reached in the case of Saifulla himself, Reshotkin was being removed from the office staff and made a fitter, and Skuryatnikov was being dismissed altogether.

An animate agent in the instrumental case may be given:

Де́ти ча́сто балу́ются роди́телями.
(Ushakov, Толко́вый слова́рь ру́сского языка́)

Children are often spoilt by their parents.

The above examples show that the reflexive-form passive can express both basic meanings of the imperfective aspect: (1) process-duration, (2) repetition. Here are two more examples to illustrate this point.

---

[1] Since the use of reflexive participles is bound up with passive participles, this subject will be dealt with in detail later, in section 4.

(1) *process-duration*:

Траншея между тем постепенно засыпалась. (Trofimov, Студенты)	Meanwhile the trench was gradually being filled up.

(2) *repetition*:

За многие годы творческой жизни Веры Михайловны Инбер книги её неоднократно издавались и переиздавались. (Новые книги)	Over the many years of Vera Mikhailovna Inber's creative life her books have been published and re-published several times.

A few reflexive verbs formed from verbs which are not strictly transitive (i.e. do not take an object in the accusative, but in the dative or instrumental) can be used with passive meaning. Peshkovsky (118) gives the following examples:

он угрожается кредиторами.	he is being threatened by creditors.
он благодетельствуется мною	he is favoured by me, i.e. I am his benefactor

(угрожать and благодетельствовать take an object in the dative);

дом управляется комендантом	the house is run by a steward

(управлять takes an object in the instrumental).

в. *Limitations on the use of reflexive verbs to express the imperfective passive*

(1) In theory, the passive may be expressed by any imperfective verb formed by the addition of -ся to a transitive verb, i.e. to one which takes an object in the accusative case: встречать, 'to meet', встречаться, 'to be met'; мыть, 'to wash', мыться, 'to be washed'. In practice, however, certain groups of 'reflexive' verbs are not used to express the passive in certain contexts. In order to understand these limitations it is necessary to consider the categories into which 'reflexive' verbs can be divided. This has already been done, for example, by V. Vinogradov (1947: 629–39), and we shall follow his system with some modifications. The term 'reflexive' is used here for convenience to denote any verb which ends in -ся:

(i) Reflexive verbs proper, verbs denoting physical actions done by the subject *on* himself, such as мыться (to wash oneself), бриться (to shave), одеваться (to dress), пудриться (to powder one's face), закутываться (to wrap oneself up), мазаться (to smear oneself).

9

(ii) Reflexive verbs denoting actions not actually done *on* oneself, such as защищáться (to defend oneself), готóвиться (to prepare (oneself)), питáться (to feed (oneself)), занимáться (to occupy oneself), учи́ться (to learn).

(iii) Verbs denoting change of position: возвращáться (to return), убирáться (to go away), останáвливаться (to stop), поднимáться (to climb), катáться (to go for a drive, to roll), повóрáчиваться (to turn), нагибáться (to bend, stoop), собирáться (to gather, collect).

(iv) Verbs denoting inner, mental or emotional state: серди́ться (to be angry), рáдоваться (to be glad), весели́ться (to be merry), беспокóиться (to worry), удивля́ться (to be surprised).

(v) Verbs such as держáться, взя́ться in держáться за пери́ла (to hold on to the rail), взя́ться за рабóту (to set about the work).

(vi) Verbs in which -ся completely changes the meaning of the original transitive verb: вози́ться (to busy oneself with), слýшаться (to obey), води́ться (to consort with), носи́ться, нести́сь (to rush).

(vii) Reciprocal verbs: встречáться (to meet (each other)), здорóваться (to greet (each other)), сражáться (to fight (each other)), борóться (to wrestle (with each other)), обнимáться (to embrace (each other)), целовáться (to kiss), мири́ться (to be reconciled (with each other)).

(viii) Verbs denoting characteristic qualities: (*a*) those which may be described as passive qualities, since the subject has something done to it—пáлка сгибáется (the stick bends), я́щик выдвигáется (the drawer comes out); (*b*) those which may be described as active qualities, such as собáка кусáется (the dog bites), крапи́ва жжётся (nettles sting).

(ix) Verbs denoting visible external manifestations: белéться (to look (show) white), чернéться (to look black), зеленéться (to show up green, to appear green, to be green).

(x) Indirect reflexives where the -ся implies not a direct object (себя́) but an indirect object (себé or для себя́): e.g. стрóиться (to have a house built), уклáдываться (to pack one's things).

(xi) Verbs in which -ся makes no essential difference to the meaning: стучáться (to knock), звони́ться (to ring), свети́ться (to shine). Vinogradov and others call these verbs 'intensive', implying that the -ся intensifies the meaning.

(xii) Verbs used in impersonal constructions: мне не спи́тся

(I can't sleep), не рабо́тается (I don't feel like work), ему́ не
сиди́тся на ме́сте (he can't keep still).

(xiii) Verbs formed with a prefix (вы-, до-, за-, на-, про-, раз-)
+-ся denoting reaching a limit or going beyond it: вы́спаться
(to have a good sleep, have one's sleep out), доучи́ться (to finish
studying), застоя́ться (to stand too long), насиде́ться (to sit long
enough), проспа́ться (to sleep oneself sober, to oversleep), разо-
спа́ться (to oversleep).

(xiv) Verbs denoting 'mutual' motion, e.g. разбега́ться (to
scatter, run off in different directions), сходи́ться (to come
together, to meet), съезжа́ться (to gather).

(xv) Verbs which have no corresponding form without -ся:
e.g. боя́ться (to fear), горди́ться (to be proud), смея́ться (to
laugh), улыба́ться (to smile), гнуша́ться (to abhor).

(xvi) Verbs which express passive meaning: many verbs given
above can be used in different contexts, with passive meaning:
мы́ться (from group (i)) can mean 'to be washed', гото́виться
(ii) 'to be prepared', возвраща́ться (iii) 'to be returned',
держа́ться (v) 'to be held', стро́иться (x) 'to be built', вы-
двига́ться (viii) 'to be taken out', встреча́ться (vii) 'to be met
with'.

The system of 'reflexive' verbs in Russian is thus extremely
involved but the above categories will help us to establish some
rules for the use of reflexive verbs for the expression of the passive
voice.

(2) (a) Verbs of group (i) above, reflexive verbs proper such as
мы́ться (to wash), одева́ться (to dress), бри́ться (to shave),
причёсываться (to comb one's hair), пу́дриться (to powder one's
face).

If these verbs are used with a person as subject they are almost
always reflexive: я мо́юсь by itself means 'I wash myself', он
бре́ется means 'he is shaving' (i.e. himself).

It is not true, however, to state categorically that such verbs
used with a person subject must be reflexive. It is perfectly natural
to say:

Я бре́юсь в э́той парикма́херской   I get shaved in this barber's shop

or:

Она́ причёсывается в э́той парик-   She has her hair done at this hair-
ма́херской.   dresser's.

In the above examples the verb is not reflexive—one does not shave oneself in a barber's, but one is shaved, and one does not do one's own hair at the hairdresser's. The meaning here is clearly passive rather than reflexive.

It is true to say, however, that a Russian would not use one of these verbs with a person subject *and* an agent in the Instrumental case, i.e. he would *not* say:

*я бре́юсь э́тим парикма́хером. I am shaved by this barber.

He would invert this statement and make it active:

меня́ бре́ет э́тот парикма́хер.[1]

A Russian would also use an active construction if the subject were an animal:

ко́шку мо́ет де́вочка. the cat is being washed by the little girl.

He would not say:

*ко́шка мо́ется де́вочкой.

Thus, a rule can be devised: *reflexive verbs proper are not used with an animate subject and an animate agent to express the passive.*[2] Verbs of this group can be used with passive meaning if the subject is inanimate and an agent is named:

окно́ мо́ется рабо́чим. the window is being washed by a workman.

The reflexive idea of such a verb is so strong that окно́ мо́ется by itself sounds absurd.

(*b*) The same care must be taken with verbs of group (ii), such as защища́ться (to defend oneself), гото́виться (to prepare (oneself)), занима́ться (to occupy oneself), and of group (iii) such as возвраща́ться (to return), собира́ться (to gather, collect). These verbs too express reflexive ideas if the subject is animate:

она́ гото́вится к экза́мену. she is preparing for an examination *not* she is being prepared.

---

[1] On the subject of transformation from passive to active see below, section 5.
[2] Some grammarians do allow the use of these verbs in a manner which contradicts this rule: Де́ти причёсываются ня́ней, 'the children are having their hair combed by their nurse' (Shakhmatov: 96); ребёнок одева́ется ма́терью, 'the child is being dressed by his mother' (Galkina-Fedoruk: 159). Such examples, are, however, confined to grammar books and are not normal Russian.

пассажи́ры собира́ются на па́лубе.	the passengers are gathering on deck *not* are being gathered.
о́вцы возвраща́ются в по́ле.	the sheep are returning to the field *not* are being returned.

These verbs are not used to express the passive with animate subjects. It is somewhat unnatural to say:

она́ гото́вится к экза́мену пофе́с- сором Ивано́вым.	she is being prepared for the examination by Professor Ivanov.
о́вцы собира́ются пастухо́м.	the sheep are being gathered by the shepherd.

The reflexive undertones of these verbs are weaker than in Group (i), and therefore these sentences are possible, whereas

*он мо́ется ба́бушкой	he is being washed by his grandmother

is not. Even so, a Russian would probably render these statements by active constructions. If, however, verbs of these groups are used with inanimate subjects, then they must be passive:

кни́ги собира́ются в библиоте́ке.	the books are being collected in the library.

compare:

чита́тели собира́ются в библио- те́ке.	the readers are gathering in the library.

(*c*) Verbs of group (iv), reflexive verbs denoting inner, mental state, such as беспоко́иться (to worry), весели́ться (to be merry), серди́ться (to be angry). These verbs are not used to express the passive. The subject is always animate: e.g.

он беспоко́ится об э́том.	he is worried (i.e. worries himself) about this.

Note the use of the phrase об э́том in the above example. One cannot use an instrumental; that is, a Russian would not say *он беспоко́ится э́тим, 'he is worried *by* this'. He would say: э́то беспоко́ит его́.

Similarly he would say either он се́рдится на неё, 'he is angry at her', or она́ се́рдит его́, 'she makes him angry'. He would not say: *он се́рдится ею for 'he is angered by her'.

In the verbs му́читься, томи́ться, терза́ться, which can be used with the Instrumental case, the dividing line between reflexive and passive is indefinable:

13

| он му́чится сомне́ниями. | he is tormented by doubts, he torments himself with doubts. |
| томи́ться ожида́нием. | to be tormented by expectation, to be in an agony of suspense. |

(*d*) The verbs of group (vi), возѝться (to busy oneself with), броса́ться (to rush), носи́ться, нести́сь (to rush), води́ться (to consort with, to be found), би́ться (to fight *or* to toss, throw oneself about, e.g. in hysterics). In these verbs, it will be recalled, the addition of -ся to the transitive verb has produced a complete change of meaning (cf. возѝть, 'to convey', броса́ть, 'to throw', носи́ть, нести́, 'to carry', слу́шать, 'to listen to', води́ть, 'to lead').

For this reason care must be taken when expressing the passive 'to be conveyed', 'to be carried', 'to be thrown', 'to be listened to', 'to be led'. The reflexive forms should not be used for the passive with animate subjects and active constructions should be substituted. Он слу́шался can only mean 'he obeyed', never 'he was listened to'. Он би́лся means 'he tossed' and is not used for 'he was beaten'. This verb би́ться can be used with passive meaning with non-personal subjects:

| кру́пная ры́ба бьётся острого́ю. | a large fish is struck with a fish-gig. |

(*e*) Reciprocal verbs. The verbs of group (vii) are in fact only reciprocal when used in the plural with animate subjects:

| они́ встреча́лись. | they used to meet each other. |
| они́ целу́ются. | they kiss each other. |

Note, however, the following constructions which are not reciprocal:

он встреча́лся с ним.	he met him.
он целу́ется с ней.	he is kissing her.
они́ встреча́лись с затрудне́ниями.	they met with difficulties.

These verbs are not used with passive meaning.

It is impossible to say:

| *он встреча́лся делега́цией | he was met by a delegation |

or

| *они́ целова́лись де́вушками. | they were kissed by the girls. |

Встреча́ться meaning 'to be found', 'to occur' may, however, be used with an animate subject:

| наибо́лее кру́пные и краси́вые ба́бочки встреча́ются в тро́пиках. | the biggest and most beautiful butterflies are found (encountered, met with) in the tropics. |

The subject may be personal: В Ло́ндоне встреча́ются таки́е оригина́лы, 'such characters are encountered in London', but clearly care must be taken to avoid ambiguity.

(*f*) Passive statements expressed by reflexive verbs with an animate agent in the instrumental case tend to sound somewhat 'official' and are characteristic of official, business style:

| Э́тот текст легко́ понима́ется студе́нтами пе́рвого ку́рса. | This text is easily understood by first-year students. |

(Pul'kina and Zakhava-Nekrasova)

In ordinary speech this would be rendered by an active verb:

студе́нты легко́ понима́ют э́тот текст.

This 'official' tone is not present when no agent is expressed:

| В э́том кио́ске продаю́тся папиро́сы. | Cigarettes are sold at this kiosk. |

(Pul'kina and Zakhava-Nekrasova)

There is in general a tendency to avoid the use of the reflexive-passive with animate subjects, of the first and second person in particular, because such usage implies the participation of the subject in the action and this has reflexive undertones. Where such verbs are used with the first and second person subject, they have an 'official' tone, as in the following example, where the person addressed is being interrogated:

| В како́м ла́гере вы содержа́лись? | In which camp were you kept? |

(Fedin, Города́ и го́ды)

c. *Use of reflexive verbs to express the perfective passive*

(1) The most common means of expressing the perfective passive is быть + the past passive participle, a subject to which we shall return in the next section. Past passive participles, however, tend to describe states. In English, when we say 'the square was covered in snow', the words *was covered* probably denote a state, not an action. To describe the action we should probably say 'the square became covered in snow'. So too in Russian пло́щадь была́ покры́та сне́гом describes a state, 'the square was covered in snow', and the action *became covered* would be rendered by a perfective verb of reflexive form: пло́щадь покры́лась сне́гом.

The sentence не́бо покры́лось облака́ми could be translated by:

> the sky had become covered by clouds
> the sky has become covered by clouds
> the sky became covered by clouds
> the sky was covered by clouds
> the sky is covered by clouds

Clearly we are here dealing with an action which produced a state, the sky is or was in a state of being covered by clouds, and this has led some writers to call this reflexive construction the passive of state. This name is, however, most misleading. It is the English translation which stresses the state, whereas the Russian perfective verb, of course, denotes an action. The perfective verb, however, does stress the result of an action, and with these verbs the result of the action is a state. Nevertheless, these perfective verbs express *actions*, not *states*, which are better expressed by participles. The following examples illustrate this point further:

День почерне́л и вдруг озари́лся мига́ющей я́ростной вспы́шкой. (Panova, Серёжа)	The day grew dark and was suddenly illuminated (i.e. became lit up) by a flickering flash.

compare:

Они́ очути́лись в шёлково-шур-ша́щем, ла́сково-щеко́тном, свежо́ и горькова́то ды́шащем ли́ствен-ном шатре́. Высоко́ над их голо-ва́ми шатёр был золоти́сто озарён зака́том, а чем ни́же, тем гу́ще темне́ли су́мерки. (Panova, Серёжа)	They found themselves under a silkily rustling, tenderly caressing, freshly and pungently smelling awning of leafy branches. High above their heads the awning was illumined by the golden light of the sunset, and lower down, the darkness of twilight became thicker and thicker.
Хороша́ се́рия портре́тов колхо́з-ников, со́зданных Глазуно́вым. Ли́ца люде́й озарены́ вну́тренней красото́й. (Огонёк)	The series of portraits of kolkhoz-workers drawn by Glazunov is very fine. The people's faces are illumined by inner beauty.

The first of the above examples contains the perfective verb озари́лся, which clearly expresses an action: *became illumined*; the last two contain the participle озарённый, which clearly denotes a state.

Some grammarians argue that these constructions with perfective reflexive verbs are not passive but descriptive, and that the noun standing in the instrumental case is not really an agent. This distinction is not very helpful, however, since 'passive' and 'descriptive' are not two mutually exclusive categories.

(2) These reflexive verbs whose perfective form is used with passive meaning make up quite a large group. They may be subdivided as follows:

(a) Verbs which describe being *covered*: задёрнуться (to be drawn over), закоптиться (to be covered with soot), закрыться (to be covered, hidden), замазаться (to get soiled, dirty), застлаться (to be covered, screened), затмиться (to be eclipsed), затуманиться (to be clouded over, dimmed), затянуться, покрыться (to be covered), запылиться (to be covered in dust), застроиться (to be covered with buildings), затопиться (to be flooded), заслониться (to be screened), обволочься (to become covered).

С утра было ясно, солнечно, потом небо затянулось облаками, и пошёл серый, тихий дождь.
(Paustovsky, Рассказ о народной медицине)

It had been fine, sunny, since early morning, then the sky became covered with clouds, and grey, silent rain began to fall.

На середине реки внезапно налетел ветер, и хлынул проливной дождь. Всё закрылось сетью мечущихся нитей.
(Lavrenyov, Выстрел с Невы)

Suddenly the wind swooped on the middle of the river and torrential rain lashed down. Everything became hidden by a mesh of flying threads.

Жадов наморщил кожу на лбу, лицо его покрылось мелкими неожиданными морщинами, стало старое.
(A. N. Tolstoy, Хождение по мукам)

Zhadov wrinkled the skin on his forehead, his face became covered with little unexpected wrinkles, became old.

(b) Verbs which describe being *filled*: заполниться, наполниться ('to be filled'; выполниться and исполниться, 'to be fulfilled', may be included here), набиться (to become filled), заселиться (to be populated, tenanted), населиться (to become populated), переполниться (to become overfilled), пропитаться (to become saturated).

Всё вокруг них пропиталось гарью и копотью.
(Leonov, Дорога на океан)

Everything around them became permeated with the smell of burning and soot.

Катины глаза наполнились светом.
(A. N. Tolstoy, Хождение по мукам)

Katya's eyes became filled with light.

«Вот и я лежа́л бы тут», — поду́- | 'I too would have lain here', he
мал он, и сно́ва всё существо́ его́ | thought, and his being was again
напо́лнилось бу́рным ощуще́нием | filled with a wild feeling of life.
жи́зни.

(Polevoy, По́весть о настоя́щем
челове́ке)

(*c*) Verbs which denote being *spoilt*: затупи́ться (to become
blunted), издыря́виться (to become riddled with holes), из-
лохма́титься (to become tattered), измя́ться (to become
crumpled), износи́ться (to get worn out), изорва́ться (to be torn
to shreds, tatters), искази́ться (to be distorted), испо́ртиться (to
be spoilt), слома́ться (to be broken).

...она́ побежа́ла вниз. Слома́лся | ...she set off running downstairs. Her
каблу́к, пре́жде чем минова́лись | heel broke before she had passed all
все двена́дцать этаже́й. | twelve floors.

(Leonov, Доро́га на океа́н)

его́ хара́ктер совсе́м испо́ртился. | his character has been completely
ruined.

(*d*) Verbs which denote being *blocked*: заколоти́ться (to be
boarded up), заку́пориться (to be corked up, sealed off), за-
пруди́ться (to be dammed), заста́виться (to be blocked),
загромозди́ться (to be blocked).

о́кна заколоти́лись доска́ми. | the windows were boarded up.

ко́мната заста́вилась ме́белью. | the room was stuffed with furniture.

(*e*) Verbs which denote being *closed* (this group is akin to the
preceding group (*d*)): закры́ться (to be closed), затвори́ться (to
be closed).

дверь закры́лась. | the door was closed *or* the door
closed.

(*f*) Verbs which denote being *opened*: откры́ться, отвори́ться,
отпере́ться (to be opened).

пре́ния откры́лись. | the debate was opened.

дверь откры́лась. | the door was opened *or* the door
opened.

(*g*) Akin to the above, verbs which denote being *revealed, laid
bare, found*: откры́ться, обнару́житься (to be revealed, discovered), обнажи́ться (to be laid bare), найти́сь, отыска́ться,
сыска́ться (to be found).

нерв обнажи́лся. | the nerve was laid bare.

18

В России ещё найдутся силы. (А. N. Tolstoy, Хождение по мукам)

Strength (powers) will still be found in Russia.

Крупицы важных сведений отыскались в Центральном партийном архиве. (Огонёк)

Pieces of important information were discovered in the Central Party Archives.

(*h*) Verbs which denote being *lost*: потеряться, растеряться.

книга потерялась.

the book is lost.

(*i*) Verbs which denote being *fastened* and *unfastened*: прикрепиться (to be fastened), приклеиться (to be stuck to), приклепаться (to be riveted to), пристроиться (to be attached, built on), прибиться (to be nailed to), привинтиться (to be screwed on), открепиться (to be unfastened), отвинтиться (to be unscrewed).

крышка плотно привинтилась.

the lid was screwed on firmly.

(*j*) Verbs which denote being *cooked*: зажариться (to be fried, roasted), завариться, отвариться (to be boiled, stewed).

чай заварился.

the tea is made.

(*k*) Verbs which denote being *realized*, *fulfilled*: выполниться, исполниться, осуществиться, сбыться.

его мечта осуществилась.

his dream was realized.

(*l*) Verbs which denote being *created*, *formed*, and *destroyed*: образоваться, составиться, создаться (to be formed), установиться (to be established), уничтожиться, разрушиться (to be destroyed).

как ни был переполнен зал, сразу образовался проход от входных дверей до самого красного стола. (Leonov, Дорога на океан)

although the room was crowded, a way was made at once from the entrance right up to the red table.

Здесь великолепная картинная галерея, которая составилась после революции из частных собраний Юсупова, Щукина, Брокара. (Огонёк)

Here there is a magnificent art gallery which was formed after the revolution from the private collections of Yusupov, Shchukin and Brokar.

(*m*) Verbs which denote being *illumined* and *darkened*: осветиться, озариться (to be illumined), омрачиться (to be darkened).

Андрей повернулся к нему; лицо его осветилось розовым блеском пламени. (Trofimov, Студенты)

Andrei turned to him; his face was lit up by the pink light of the flame.

(*n*) Verbs which denote being *taken apart*: разобра́ться, разня́ться (to be taken apart), разре́заться (to be dissected).

маши́на с трудо́м разобра́лась.	the machine was stripped down with difficulty.

(*o*) Verbs which denote being *connected* and *disconnected*, *separated*: соедини́ться, скрепи́ться (to be connected), разъедини́ться (to be disconnected).

концы́ верёвок соедини́лись/разъедини́лись.	the ends of the ropes were connected/disconnected.

(*p*) Verbs which denote being *distributed, divided, set apart*: e.g. распредели́ться, расста́виться, раздви́нуться

сту́лья расста́вились.	the chairs were set out.

In addition to the above groups, the following perfective reflexive verbs with passive meaning are frequently encountered:

смени́ться (to be replaced, superseded):

Уже́ че́рез не́сколько шаго́в э́то чу́вство смени́лось обы́чным челове́ческим смуще́ньем. (Leonov, Доро́га на океа́н)	Within a few steps this feeling was replaced by the usual human embarrassment.

потре́боваться (to be required, demanded):

Потре́буется огро́мное мора́льное и физи́ческое напряже́ние. (Огонёк)	Great moral and physical effort will be required.

сохрани́ться (to be preserved):

Ста́рое зда́ние хорошо́ сохрани́лось.	The old building has been well preserved.

послы́шаться (to be heard):

послы́шались шаги́.	footsteps were heard.

вспо́мниться (to be recalled):

мне вспо́мнилось, что...	I remembered that...

The above list of perfective verbs is not exhaustive. There are many other reflexive verbs whose perfective form may be used in this way: просла́виться (to become famous, to be famed), смягчи́ться (to be softened), отрази́ться (to be reflected), обогати́ться (to be enriched), укра́ситься (to be adorned, beautified).

In general, it will be observed, these verbs denote change of state and they are required because the more usual perfective passive (быть + the past participle passive) would convey not the action of becoming changed, but the state of having been changed: compare

Воздух был пропитан холодным запахом мокрых доцветающих трав.	The air was filled with the cold smell of damp, fading weeds.
(Paustovsky, Соловьиное царство)	

and

Всё вокруг них пропиталось гарью и копотью.	Everything around them became permeated with the smell of burning and soot.
(Leonov, Дорога на океан)	

The past participles of the verbs discussed above may be used to express the idea of *having become*..., e.g.

Он с готовностью прикладывал губы к стеклу, затуманившемуся от маминого дыхания...	He eagerly pressed his lips to the glass which had become clouded from his mother's breath...
(Panova, Серёжа)	

(3) Some observations on the use of these perfective reflexive verbs are necessary:

(a) They are not used with an animate agent, i.e. it is *not* possible to say: *библиотека открылась библиотекарем for 'the library was opened by the librarian'. This statement must be rendered by: библиотека была открыта библиотекарем or библиотеку открыл библиотекарь. If we say: библиотека была открыта and do not name an agent, we are referring to a state: 'the library was open'. If we add an agent, библиотекарем, we turn была открыта into an action: библиотека была открыта библиотекарем. The perfective reflexive verbs are thus needed to denote a passive action only if an animate agent is not given. If he is included, then быть + past participle passive is possible (and indeed necessary), because there can hardly be any possibility of describing a state instead of an action.

(b) Such verbs may be used with animate subjects:

Катя покрылась, наконец, испариной.	Katya at last became covered with perspiration.
(A. N. Tolstoy, Хождение по мукам)	

4. THE USE OF PASSIVE PARTICIPLES

There are three passive participles in Russian, two imperfective and one perfective. They are the present passive participle (читаемый, любимый), the imperfective past participle passive (писанный, виденный) and the perfective past participle passive (написанный, увиденный).

A. *The use of the present passive participle*

(1) Contrary to what many textbooks of Russian imply, the present passive participle is widely and frequently used. Not all Russian verbs, however, have this participle. It is formed only from:

(*a*) Regular first conjugation verbs and those in -авать, e.g. читаемый (read), возглавляемый (headed, led), даваемый (given).

(*b*) Unprefixed verbs in -овать, организуемый (organized), атакуемый (attacked).

(*c*) The verbs of motion носить, водить, возить and their compounds: носимый (carried), привозимый (brought). The participles несомый from нести and ведомый from вести are now archaic, though ведомый has certain specialized modern uses.

(*d*) Only some verbs of the second conjugation, the following being in general use: томимый (tormented), ценимый (valued, respected), любимый (loved), хранимый (preserved, kept), терпимый (suffered, allowed, borne), слышимый (heard), гонимый (pursued). Note also from двигать (first conjugation) движимый (moved).

(*e*) Verbs of the first conjugation which form their present tense with insertion of л: трепать–треплет–треплемый (flapped, tapped, tugged), колеблемый (moved).

A number of present passive participles from verbs which are not strictly transitive (i.e. do not take an object in the accusative case) are in common use: руководимый (led), управляемый (managed, ruled), предшествуемый (preceded), сопутствуемый (accompanied), угрожаемый (threatened), командуемый (commanded).

(2) The short form of the present passive participle is sometimes used with быть to describe a passive action. Vinogradov (640) compares the statements по́ле вспа́хивалось колхо́зниками and по́ле бы́ло вспа́хиваемо колхо́зниками, which may both be translated as 'the field was ploughed up' or 'was being ploughed up by the collective farmers'. There is, however, a difference of emphasis in these two statements. Whilst both may refer to single or repeated events, the participle construction stresses in particular the passive state of the subject, emphasizes the idea of the subject's being temporarily subjected to the action.

This same idea, however, can be expressed by a reflexive verb, especially with the help of an adverb, as in:

транше́я ме́жду тем постепе́нно засыпа́лась	meanwhile the trench was gradually being filled up.

Thus, the use of the present passive participle in this way with быть is quite rare. It is normally found where the reflexive verb would be impossible or better avoided:

Лео́нтий Наза́рович всю жизнь был обурева́ем вели́кой мечто́й... (Paustovsky, Усну́вший ма́льчик)	All his life Leontii Nazarovich was excited by a great dream...

(the reflexive form обурева́лся is not used).

все они́ люби́ли кого́-то и бы́ли люби́мы. (Trofimov, Студе́нты)	they all loved somebody and were loved

(они́ люби́лись would mean 'they were having a love affair').

Судьбо́ю я был неоднокра́тно поставля́ем в разли́чные столкнове́ния. (Leonov, Доро́га на океа́н)	More than once I found myself being placed by Fate in various conflicts.

(In this example the participial construction particularly stresses the idea of the passive process; the reflexive verb is avoided also because of possible reflexive undertones.)

To stress the repetitive idea, быва́ть may be used instead of быть with the present passive participle:

Он иногда́ исчеза́л на ме́сяцы и, возвраща́ясь, быва́л встреча́ем о́пять той же улы́бкой.	He would sometimes disappear for months and, on returning, would be met by the same smile. (W. A. Morison, *Studies in Russian Forms and Uses*, 43)

(3) The present passive participle is most frequently used as an attribute: кни́га, чита́емая все́ми or чита́емая все́ми кни́га (the book being read by everybody).

In such cases it expresses an action simultaneous with the action of the main verb:

И тепе́рь, подгоня́емый тече́нием собы́тий, торопи́лся сам.
(Leonov, Доро́га на океа́н)

And now, driven on by the course of events, he himself was in a hurry.

Ухвати́вшись за коне́ц, ослеплённый бры́згами, сбива́емые волно́й, тащи́ли бот к бе́регу.
(Lavrenyov, Со́рок пе́рвый)

Grasping the rope, blinded by the spray and being continually knocked down by the wave(s), they dragged the boat towards the shore.

смерть Никола́я Ива́новича ли́шний раз подтвержда́ет пра́вильность агра́рной поли́тики, проводи́мой его па́ртией.
(A. N. Tolstoy, Хожде́ние по му́кам)

the death of Nikolai Ivanovich confirms once more the correctness of the agrarian policy being carried out by his party.

Она́ ду́мала о своём далёком му́же, неве́домо где носи́мом вое́нными ве́трами.
(Polevoy, По́весть о настоя́щем челове́ке)

She thought of her husband far away, carried she knew not where by the winds of war.

Охраня́емый На́стей бага́ж ку́чей лежа́л у скамьи́.
(S. Antonov, Алёнка)

The luggage that Nastya was guarding lay in a heap by the bench.

The use of participles is complicated by the existence of reflexive participles which may have passive meaning: it is possible to say кни́га, чита́ющаяся все́ми as well as кни́га, чита́емая все́ми. The construction кни́га, чита́юшаяся все́ми is, of course, the participle equivalent of кни́га, кото́рая чита́ется все́ми, whilst кни́га, чита́емая все́ми is the equivalent of кни́га, кото́рую все чита́ют. Stylistically both of these participle constructions are elevated and would not be used in speech. The following examples have been taken from works on Russian grammar which are mentioned below in the Bibliography (p. 46):

Вероя́тно, таки́х «окказиона́льных» слов, употребля́емых в ре́чи ре́дко, то́лько при подходя́щих ситуа́циях, име́ется мно́го со́тен, е́сли не ты́сяч.
(F. P. Filin, О двух значе́ниях глаго́лов)

Probably there are many hundreds, if not thousands of such nonce-words, used rarely in speech, only in suitable contexts.

24

Большинство учёных считали их	Most scholars have considered them
осо́быми слова́ми, употребля́ю-	to be special words used in the func-
щимися в фу́нкции сказу́емого...	tion of a predicate...

In these two statements the participles употребля́емый and употребля́ющийся are interchangeable.

This does not mean, however, that in translating a sentence which requires a participle expressing action simultaneous with the main verb the student may choose freely between a present passive or a present reflexive participle. The following rules can be devised:

(*a*) The reflexive participle must, of course, be used where the verb has no present passive participle:

дом, стро́ящийся на углу́ у́лицы.	the house being built at the corner of the street (there is no participle *строимый).

(*b*) The reflexive participle should be avoided if it is formed from one of those groups of verbs where the reflexive usually has truly reflexive meaning: i.e. one should avoid saying:

*ребёнок, одева́ющийся ма́терью.	the child being dressed by his mother.

(In this case the passive participle must be used: ребёнок, одева́емый ма́терью.)

Even if the verb in question has no present passive participle, the reflexive should not be used; for example мыть (to wash) has no present passive participle, but the statement 'the child being washed by his mother' should be transformed into an active statement (ребёнок, кото́рого мать мо́ет), and not rendered by the reflexive participle (i.e. one should not say *ребёнок, мо́ющийся ма́терью).

In other words, the restrictions on the use of reflexive verbs to express the passive outlined in 3 B above, should be observed in the use of participles.

(*c*) It has been observed above that the passive idea of the subject as the temporary recipient of an action is stronger with the present passive participle than with a reflexive verb, and this extends to the present reflexive participle. Where a straight choice between a present passive participle and a reflexive participle has to be made, the passive participle is used to emphasize the passive action itself; when the reflexive participle is used, the passive action itself is of lesser importance than some other element of the phrase, such as an adverb or adverbial phrase. In practice the reflexive participle tends to denote some general, permanent characteristic:

Изучáя егó архи́в, храня́щийся в Отдéле рýкописей Госудáрственной Третьякóвской галерéи, а тáкже другие материáлы, удалóсь установи́ть, что Верещáгин был на Кýбе в течéние 1902 гóда двáжды. (Огонёк)

By studying his archives, kept in the Department of Manuscripts of the State Tret'yakov Gallery, and also other materials, it was possible to establish that Vereshchagin was twice in Cuba in 1902.

Развора́чивая кáждое ýтро «Вéстник Самáрского совéта», печáтающийся на обёрточной бумáге, (он) сти́скивал чéлюсти. (A. N. Tolstoy, Хождéние по мýкам)

Opening every morning *The Bulletin of the Samara Soviet*, (which was) printed on wrapping paper, he would clench his teeth.

In both of these examples the antecedent is not being subjected to a temporary action. In the case of Vereshchagin's archives, the fact that the archives are being preserved is of less significance than the place where they are kept; and the fact that *The Bulletin of the Samara Soviet* is being printed is not so significant as the kind of paper of which it is made.

The present passive participle, however, emphasizes that the antecedent is being subjected to a particular action or set of actions, and the passive action itself is of prime significance:

Голóдный, расхищáемый дерéвнями, насквóзь прохвáченный поля́рным вéтром Петербýрг, окружённый неприя́тельским фрóнтом, сотрясáемый зáговорами, гóрод без угля́ и хлéба, с погáсшими трýбами завóдов, гóрод, как обнажённый мозг человéческий, — излучáл в э́то врéмя радиоволнáми Царскосéльской стáнции бéшеные взры́вы идéй. (A. N. Tolstoy, Хождéние по мýкам)

Hungry, (being) robbed by the villages, pierced through and through by the arctic wind, St Petersburg, encircled by the enemy's front line, (being) shaken by plots, the city without coal and bread, its factory chimneys still, the city, like a bared human brain, radiated at that time furious explosions of ideas on the radio waves of the Tsarskoe Selo broadcasting station.

Слы́шно бы́ло, как повизгивала рýчка кофéйной мéленки и гремéла посýда, небрéжно сдвигáемая с плиты́. (Leonov, Дорóга на океáн)

One could hear the handle of the coffee-mill squeaking and the utensils rattling as they were carelessly taken from the cooker.

Since there is a general tendency to avoid the reflexive passive with animate agents the present passive participle is normally preferable when an agent is named:

...только сильные лучи фар, простреливаемые раскалёнными мошками, раздвигали темноту.
(S. Antonov, Алёнка)

...only the powerful rays of the head-lights, shot through by incandescent midges, pierced the darkness.

Тогда атаман Каледин обратился к Дону с последним безнадёжным призывом — послать казаков-добровольцев в единственное стойкое военное образование — в добровольческую армию, формируемую в Ростове генералами Корниловым, Алексеевым и Деникиным.
(A. N. Tolstoy, Хождение по мукам)

Then ataman Kaledin turned to the Don with a last hopeless call to send volunteer Cossacks to the only firm military organization, to the volunteer army being formed in Rostov by Generals Kornilov, Alekseev and Denikin.

B. *The use of the imperfective past passive participle*

(1) The following is a list of imperfective past passive participles found in modern literary Russian. Some highly technical words have been omitted; so too have participles formed from those verbs which may be either imperfective or perfective, e.g. меблированный (furnished). The words in brackets are adjectives.

белённый	whitened
битый	beaten, smashed
бритый	shaved
варенный (варёный)	boiled, stewed
виданный and виденный	seen
витый	twisted, curled
воронённый (воронёный)	burnished
вощённый (вощёный)	waxed
газированный	aerated
глаженный (глаженый)	smoothed, ironed
глоданный	gnawed
гнутый	bent
говорённый	spoken
грабленный	plundered, robbed
гранённый (гранёный)	cut
гримированный	made-up, painted
груженный (гружёный)	loaded, laden
давленный	crushed
деланный	made
держанный	held (держаный, 'used, second-hand')
долблённый	hollowed out, chiselled
дроблённый (дроблёный)	fractured, divided
дубленный (дублёный)	tanned
жаренный (жареный)	roasted, fried
жатый	pressed

жа́тый	reaped
жёванный	chewed
жела́нный	desired
зва́нный	called, invited
и́гранный	played
ква́шенный (ква́шеный)	leavened
кипячённый (кипячёный)	boiled
кле́енный (клеёный)	gummed
клёпанный (клёпаный)	riveted
ко́ванный	forged, shod (ко́ваный, 'beaten, reinforced with iron')
коксо́ванный	coked
конопа́ченный (конопа́ченый)	caulked
концентри́рованный	concentrated
копчённый (копчёный)	smoked
ко́рмленный	fed (ко́рмленый, 'fattened')
кра́денный (кра́деный)	stolen
кра́шенный (кра́шеный)	coloured, painted
кручённый (кручёный)	twisted
кры́тый	covered
лакиро́ванный	varnished
ле́ченный	treated, healed
ли́занный	licked
лино́ванный (лино́ваный)	lined
ли́тый	poured, cast
лицо́ванный	faced
ло́вленный	caught
ло́манный (ло́маный)	broken
лощённый (лощёный)	polished, glossy
лужённый (лужёный)	tinned
лу́пленный	skinned, peeled
лущённый	shelled, podded
ма́занный (ма́заный)	smeared
ме́ченный (ме́ченый)	marked
моло́ченный (моло́ченый)	threshed
морённый (морёный)	fumed, stained
моро́женный (моро́женый)	frozen
мо́ченный (мочёный)	soaked
мощённый (мощёный)	paved
мура́вленный (мура́вленый)	glazed
мы́тый	washed
мя́тый	crumpled, crushed
надёванный	worn, old
но́шенный	carried
па́ренный (па́реный)	steamed
патрули́рованный	patrolled
па́хтанный	churned
па́чканный (па́чканый)	dirtied
пемзо́ванный	pumice-stoned
пе́тый	sung

печа́танный	printed
печённый (печёный)	baked
пи́ленный (пилёный)	sawn
пи́санный (пи́саный)	written, painted
пи́тый	drunk
пла́вленный (пла́вленый)	smelted
плани́рованный	planned
плетённый (плетёный)	woven
пломбиро́ванный	filled (of teeth)
по́енный (поёный)	watered, given to drink
полиро́ванный	polished
по́лотый	weeded
по́ротый	unpicked, undone
по́рченный	spoilt
пра́вленный (пра́вленый)	corrected
про́шенный	asked
пы́танный	tortured
ре́занный (ре́заный)	cut
рифмо́ванный	rhymed
ру́бленный (ру́бленый)	chopped, minced
ры́тый	dug
са́женный (са́женый)	set
серебрённый (серебрёный)	silvered
слащённый (слащёный)	sweetened
слы́шанный	heard
смо́тренный	seen
со́санный	sucked
ста́вленный	put
стёганный (стёганый)	padded, quilted
сти́ранный (сти́раный)	washed, cleaned
стри́женный (стри́женый)	cut short (of hair)
су́шенный (сушёный)	dried
сы́панный	sprinkled
та́сканный	pulled
тёртый	rubbed, grated
тёсанный (тёсаный)	hewn
тка́нный (тка́ный)	woven
томлённый (томлёный)	stewed
то́пленный (топлёный)	heated
то́ченный (точёный)	sharpened
тракто́ванный	treated
трениро́ванный	trained
трёпанный	shaken, pulled, frayed
трети́рованный	treated
тушёванный	shaded
у́ченный	taught, learnt (учёный, 'learned'; as noun, 'scholar')
фарширо́ванный	stuffed
хлёстанный	whipped
це́женный	strained

целóванный	kissed
чёсанный (чёсаный)	combed
чи́ненный	mended
чи́танный	read
чи́щенный (чи́щеный)	cleaned
ши́тый	sewn, embroidered
шлифóванный	polished
шнурóванный	laced
штампóванный	stamped
штемпелёванный	stamped
штóпанный (штóпаный)	darned
штрафóванный	fined
штрихóванный	shaded
штуди́рованный	studied
штукату́ренный	plastered
щи́панный	pinched, nipped
экзаменóванный	examined
эксплоати́рованный	exploited
эмалирóванный	enamelled.

(2) The imperfective past passive participle is rarely used in its short form with быть, in such phrases as был чи́тан, to form a passive conjugation. In modern literary Russian it usually adds a colloquial or archaic tone to the passage:

На Лóбное мéсто, где лежáл когдá-то нагишóм...уби́тый Лжедими́трий, откýда выкри́кивали и ски́дывали царéй, откýда чи́таны бы́ли все вóльности и все вóли нарóда рýсского,...взошёл солдáтик.
(A. N. Tolstoy, Хождéние по мýкам)

On to the Place of Execution, where once there lay naked the slain Pretender Dimitry, from where they called out and deposed Russian tsars, from where were read out all rights and liberties of the people of Russia...there climbed a little soldier.

In this example it would have been normal to write откýда читáлись все вóльности...but this would have lacked the deliberately archaic flavour of чи́таны бы́ли.

The same construction is used for the same effect in

Ещё во временá Петрá Пéрвого дьячóк от Трóицкой цéркви... уви́дел кики́мору — худýю бáбу и простоволóсую, — си́льно испугáлся и затéм кричáл в кабакé: «Петербýргу, мол, быть пустý», — за что был схвáчен, пы́тан в Тáйной канцеля́рии и бит кнутóм нещáдно.
(A. N. Tolstoy, Хождéние по мýкам)

In the time of Peter the Great a sacristan of the Church of the Trinity saw an unclean spirit, a woman thin and bareheaded, was exceedingly terrified and shouted later in an inn, 'St Petersburg will be deserted'—for which he was seized, tortured in the Secret Chancery and mercilessly beaten with the knout.

In the above sentence, however, the imperfective reflexive passive would be avoided because both пытáться and бúться have other possible meanings; пытáться, 'to attempt', бúться, 'to fight, toss', etc. The normal way of expressing this statement in modern Russian would be by means of an active construction.

Imperfective past passive participles are occasionally used for colloquial effect where the perfective past passive participle would be normal in literary style:

Когдá повернýл бревнó — запúс-ка. Наклéена глáдко рúжим тéс-том. Пúсана чернúльным каран-дашóм. (Fedin, Городá и гóды)	When he turned over the log—a note. Stuck on flat with reddish paste. Written with an indelible pencil.
Рыбáчью хибáру нашлá. Чúстый дворéц! Сухáя, крéпкая, дáже в óкнах стёкла не бúты. (Lavrenyov, Сóрок пéрвый)	She found a fisherman's cottage. A perfect palace! Dry, solid, even the window-panes were not broken.

(3) The imperfective past passive participle is often used in this way with a negative, e.g.

пол не мыт	the floor has not been washed
бельё не глáжено	the washing has not been ironed
мой носкú не чúнены	my stockings have not been mended

In these sentences the participle has no archaic flavour and does not sound particularly colloquial, although these are statements which normally occur in conversation. The perfective participle would be used for the positive.

(4) Imperfective past passive participles may also be used attributively to refer to imperfective actions previous to the main verb. In such constructions they are not archaic or colloquial:

...послéдней мúслью васыпáю-щего Алексéя былá стрáнная мысль о том, что...всё это из чудéсной кнúжки, чúтанной в дéтстве в далёком гóроде Камúшине. (Polevoy, Пóвесть о настоýщем человéке)	Alexei's last thought as he fell asleep was the strange idea that all this was from a wonderful book read in childhood in the far-off town of Kamyshin.
Чéрез час, утомлённой всем вúден-ным, он выхóдит на своéй любúмой стáнции. (Trofimov, Студéнты)	An hour later, worn out by all he had seen, he got out at his favourite station.
И тепéрь Вадúм вспóмнил слú-шанные им в дéтстве словá отцá о воспитáнии людéй — нóвых лю-дéй, борцóв за коммунúзм. (Trofimov, Студéнты)	And now Vadim recalled the words he used to hear in his childhood from his father about the creation of new people, fighters for communism.

31

The participles ви́денный, слы́шанный and чи́танный are the most frequently used in this way. Otherwise, in order to express imperfective actions previous to the main verb, the past reflexive participle is used:

сочине́ние, писа́вшееся тогда́ студе́нтом, тепе́рь лежи́т пе́ред на́ми.

the essay being written by the student at that time now lies before us.

The usual restrictions on the use of the reflexive verbs apply. Here are more examples of this usage:

Вме́сте с на́ми все че́стные лю́ди подде́рживают тре́бование о наказа́нии уби́йц, с кото́рым уже́ обрати́лись в суде́бные о́рганы ФРГ това́рищи из объедине́ния лиц, пресле́довавшихся при фаши́зме. (Огонёк)

Together with us, all honest people support the demand for the punishment of the murderers which has been submitted to the judicial organs of the Federal Republic of Germany by comrades from the organization of people persecuted under Fascism.

Изве́стно, что во мно́гих слу́чаях слова́, употребля́вшихся в литерату́рном языке́ с да́внего вре́мени, по тем или ины́м причи́нам не помеща́лись в пре́жних словаря́х. (Filin, О двух значе́ниях глаго́лов...)

It is well known that in many cases, words used in the literary language since early times were not included for some reason in earlier dictionaries.

Он привёз сюда́ кни́ги, сохраня́вшиеся где-то в прови́нции. (Leonov, Доро́га на океа́н)

He brought here books which had been kept somewhere in the provinces.

The imperfective past reflexive participle is sometimes used instead of the present reflexive participle to express action contemporaneous with the main verb, e.g.

В после́дние дни в Петрогра́де произошли́ беспоря́дки, сопровожда́вшиеся наси́лием. (A. N. Tolstoy, Хожде́ние по му́кам)

In the last few days in Petrograd there have occurred disorders accompanied by violence...

Осо́бое внима́ние привлекли́ экспони́ровавшиеся на вы́ставке карти́ны инди́йской се́рии и ру́сско-туре́цкой войны́ 1877–1878 годо́в. (Огонёк)

His attention was attracted particularly by the pictures of the Indian series and of the Russo-Turkish War of 1877–1878 (which were) being shown at the exhibition.

The use of a past participle where a present participle might be expected is not confined to reflexive participles, of course. It is part of a wider problem which cannot be examined here. However, W. A. Morison (*Slavonic and East European Review*, XLII, 299) has put forward the view that the past participle is used in this way if no logical emphasis falls on the activity, i.e. if the action is what would be expected and does not need to have the attention drawn to it, e.g.

девушка, сидевшая на скамейке	the girl who was sitting on the bench

but

девушка, стоящая на скамейке.	the girl who was standing on the bench.

This explanation would hold good for the examples given in this section.

(5) The imperfective past passive participle is most frequently used as an adjective, e.g. крытая повозка, 'a covered wagon', i.e. the type of wagon that is covered, not a wagon which happens to have been covered by somebody.

битая посуда два века живёт.	cracked crocks last for ever.
У него было загорелое лицо, бритое и простоватое. (Leonov, Дорога на океан)	He had a sunburnt face, clean-shaven and somewhat simple.

Many imperfective past passive participles formed with -нный lose an н when they become adjectivalized, so that, for example, писанный ('written') becomes писаный:

писаный документ	a written document
укрыватель краденого	receiver of stolen goods
жареное мясо	roast meat
печёный картофель	baked potato

The form ending in -нный is thus to be regarded as the participle proper; the form in -ный is an adjective, cf.

печёный картофель	baked potato
картофель, печённый в золе	potato baked in ashes

Occasionally a past participle formed from an imperfective intransitive verb, e.g. сижено, работано, is found, but these are only used in literary Russian for colloquial effect:

много работано.	a lot of work has been done (over a long period).

c. *The use of the perfective past passive participle*

(1) The perfective passive is normally rendered by the appropriate form of быть and the perfective past passive participle in its short form: this expresses the result of an action. The verb быть may be in the past tense:

Статья была написана по-русски.
(Leonov, Дорога на океан)

The article was written in Russian.

К концу 1834 года повесть была написана и в 1835 году напечатана в «Миргороде».
(S. M. Petrov, История русского романа)

The story was written towards the end of 1834, and in 1835 it was printed in *Mirgorod* (a reference to Gogol's Тарас Бульба.)

or the verb быть may be in the future tense:

Господа, прошу вас расходиться по домам. Ваши просьбы будут рассмотрены.
(A. N. Tolstoy, Хождение по мукам)

Ladies and gentlemen, I beg you to go to your homes. Your requests will be examined.

Он заранее знает, какое слово будет произнесено.
(Panova, Серёжа)

He knows in advance what word will be spoken.

or, if the participle describes a state obtaining at the present time, it may stand alone:

Очень скверно освещены в Москве дорожные знаки.   (Огонёк)

The road signs in Moscow are very badly lit.

Притом же коньяк выпит, время позднее и хозяева хотят спать.
(Leonov, Дорога на океан)

Besides, the cognac is all drunk, the hour is late and the hosts want to sleep.

or the participle may be used with the gerund будучи:

Будучи дважды ранен, Чупахин не оставил своего оружия.
(Огонёк)

Although wounded twice, Chupakhin did not leave his weapon.

or the participle may be used with the infinitive быть. In this case the participle may be short:

Жизнь человеческая должна быть украшена.
(Paustovsky, Уснувший мальчик)

Human life must be beautified.

Работы, удостоенные золотой медалью, должны быть напечатаны.
(Огонёк)

Works honoured with a gold medal should be printed.

34

То есть, ты дýмала, что я мог быть убúт? (Fedin, Горóда и гóды)

That is, you thought I might be killed?

Конéчно, не все их твóрческие зáмыслы мóгут быть претворенú в жизнь. (Огонёк)

Of course, not all their creative ideas can be put into effect.

or, the participle may be in the long instrumental form after the infinitive быть (and often is when the infinitive is not used with the auxiliaries дóлжен and мочь).

А нельзя́ ли и мне быть посвящённым в причúну сих слёз? (А. N. Tolstoy, Хождéние по мýкам)

And may I not be initiated into the reason for these tears?

...он положúл самолёт на обрáтный курс, к лúнии фрóнта, к свойм, чтóбы в слýчае чегó хотя́ бы быть похоронённым роднúми людьмú. (Polevoy, Пóвесть о настоя́щем человéке)

...he set the aircraft on a return course, towards the front line, towards his own side, so that if anything happened to him, he would at least be buried by his own people.

After such words as казáться (to seem), окáзываться (to prove to be) the participle is used in the long instrumental form as an adjective would be:

По утрáм листóчки э́ти сверкáли на сóлнце и казáлись вúрезанными из компрéссной бумáги. (Polevoy, Пóвесть о настоя́щем человéке)

In the mornings these leaves shone in the sun and seemed cut out of compressed paper.

...пóле оказáлось изрúтым глубóкими ухáбами. (Nagibin, Подсáдная ýтка)

...the field turned out to be pitted with deep holes.

The difficulties which surround the use of the imperfective reflexive passive, of course, do not apply to the perfective passive formed with быть and the perfective past passive participle. It is perfectly natural to say ребёнок был вúмыт мáтерью for 'the child was washed by his mother'. However, there is sometimes a need to use the perfective reflexive passive because the perfective participle passive tends to express a state.

(2) The short form of the perfective passive participle is used with бывáть to describe a repeated state:

...стáрый особня́к на Фонтáнке, где помещáлось óбщество по суб-

...the old detached house on the Fontanka where the society was

ботам, в дни открытых заседаний, бывал переполнен.
(А. N. Tolstoy, Хождение по мукам)

located used to be crowded on Saturdays, the days of the open sessions.

Уже приобрёл анекдотическую известность ресторан в городе Гусь-Хрустальном, который бывал закрыт от трёх до четырёх часов дня на обеденный перерыв.
(Огонёк)

Already the restaurant in Gus'-Khrustal'ny which used to be closed for lunch from three till four in the afternoon has achieved anecdotal notoriety.

Однако, общим для них является тот факт, что их выставки крайне неохотно посещаются (за исключением первого дня, когда бывают приглашены сильные мира сего — возможные покупатели).
(Огонёк)

However, common to all of them is the fact that their exhibitions are visited extremely reluctantly (except for the first day when are invited the mighty of this world—the possible buyers).

(3) There is a tendency for the perfective past passive participle to become adjectivalized. In this first example the word воспитанный is used as a participle:

она хорошо воспитана

she has been well brought up

whereas in this second example it is an adjective:

она воспитанна.

she is educated *or* refined.

Note the double нн in the adjective. Other common words which play this dual role are образованный (formed, educated), ограниченный (limited), сдержанный (restrained).

It will be observed that the boundary between participle and adjective may be very difficult to define and, since there is a growing tendency for the adjective to be used in the long nominative form as a complement, instances of the use of the participle in the long nominative form after быть can be found:

...тут крыша вся начисто побитая осколками.
(Sholokhov, Судьба человека)

...here the roof has been completely shattered by shrapnel.

«У меня рука вдребезги разбитая, а ты её так и рванул». Слышу, он засмеялся потихоньку и говорит, «...А рука у тебя не разбита, а выбита была, вот я её на место поставил».
(Sholokhov, Судьба человека)

'My arm is smashed to bits and you gave it such a tug.' I heard him chuckle quietly and say, 'Your arm wasn't broken but dislocated, and I've put it back in place.'

36

Па́па был весь перема́занный, у него́ тогда́ не заводи́лся тра́ктор. И лицо́ и ру́ки у па́пы бы́ли вы́мазаны чёрным ма́слом.
(S. Antonov, Алёнка)

Daddy was smeared all over, his tractor wouldn't start. Daddy's face and his hands were smeared in black oil.

In all these examples the participle is used with весь (all) or вдре́безги (completely, to pieces), but the short form could be used with these words, and normally would be: па́па был весь перема́зан.

In the following example the long nominative form of the participle follows two adjectives in the long form:

Мо́ре бы́ло вы́цветшее, бле́дно-голубо́е и то́лько ко́е-где вдалеке́ тро́нутое ма́товой ря́бью.
(A. N. Tolstoy, Хожде́ние по му́кам)

The sea was faded, pale-blue, and only here and there in the distance touched by a lustreless ripple.

This does not mean, however, that a participle must be long if used after long adjectives in this way, as the following quotation from the same source shows:

Широкоску́лые ли́ца солда́т бы́ли уста́лые и покры́ты пы́лью.

The broad faces of the soldiers were tired and covered in dust.

It is recommended that the student take note of this usage but in practice use the short form of the participle after a finite form of быть, i.e. after был, бу́дет or the verb *to be* 'understood' in the present tense.

5. EXPRESSION OF PASSIVE IDEAS BY ACTIVE CONSTRUCTIONS

In the course of this discussion of ways of expressing the passive it has often been said that certain passive constructions would be avoided in Russian and that the idea would be expressed by an active construction: e.g.

ребёнка мо́ет мать.

the child is washed by his mother.

In the above example the reflexive passive мо́ется should not be used, but even where a passive construction is perfectly acceptable in Russian, an active construction may well be used instead of it. In fact, literary Russian in general uses far fewer passive constructions than English, though they are much commoner in technical Russian where experiments and processes are described.

The ways in which this 'conversion' from passive to active may be effected are as follows:

(1) Where the action is performed by a named animate agent (the child was being washed by his mother) the agent becomes the subject in Russian and the subject of the English sentence becomes the object after a transitive verb; usually the object is placed before the verb and the subject after it:

Его́ высоко́ цени́л В. В. Ста́сов, кото́рый посвяти́л карти́нам Пря́нишникова мно́го стате́й.
(Огонёк)

He was highly regarded by V. V. Stasov, who devoted many articles to Pryanishnikov's pictures.

Так ещё до появле́ния И́мре на свет, его́ спасли́ сове́тские солда́ты.
(Огонёк)

And so even before his appearance in the world Imre was saved by Soviet troops.

In the above examples an active statement could be used in English, but it is more natural and stylistically preferable in English to use the passive. In the first example it would sound rather stilted Russian to say он высоко́ цени́лся Ста́совым but in the second it would have been quite possible to say он был спасён сове́тскими солда́тами.

(2) The same construction may be used if the action is produced not by an animate agent but by some inanimate agency or instrument:

Меня́ развесели́ла наи́вность, с како́й вы зева́ли на балага́ны.
(Fedin, Города́ и го́ды)

I was amused by the naivety with which you were gaping at the booths.

Ма́ри — дочь У́рбаха, Ге́нрих-Адо́льф — сын фрау У́рбах, урождённой фон Фре́йлебен. Их соединя́ли то́лько и́мя и столо́вая... Они́ бы́ли чужи́ми.
(Fedin, Города́ и го́ды)

Mary was the daughter of Urbach, Heinrich-Adolf—the son of Frau Urbach, *née* von Freileben. They were united only by their name and by the dining-room...They were strangers.

(3) If the action is performed by an unspecified human agency an impersonal construction with the verb in the third person plural is used, even if it is likely that the action is performed only by one person.

Пусть лю́ди зна́ют, за что сня́ли профе́ссора.
(Trofimov, Студе́нты)

Let people know why the professor was removed.

Ра́зве я когда́-нибудь тре́бовал, чтобы меня́ весели́ли и забавля́ли?
(Karavayeva, Гра́ни жи́зни)

Have I ever demanded that I should be cheered and amused.

(4) If the action described is one of damage or injury caused by an inanimate agency or instrument, the verb is put into the third person singular (neuter):

Ему́ пу́шечным огнём глаза́ вы́жгло. (Paustovsky, Разли́вы рек)	His eyes were burnt out by machine-gun fire.
...как то́лько услы́шал э́ти слова́, — меня́ бу́дто огнём обожгло́. (Sholokhov, Судьба́ челове́ка)	...as soon as I heard these words, it was as if I were scorched with fire.
Прониза́ло меня́, бу́дто электри́ческим то́ком, потому́ почу́ял я недо́брое. (Sholokhov, Судьба́ челове́ка)	I was pierced as if by an electric current because I sensed misfortune.

(5) This third person singular impersonal construction is frequently used to describe an 'act of God'.

Мост че́рез Нере́дицу снесло́ полово́дьем. (Paustovsky, Беспоко́йство)	The bridge over the Nereditsa has been swept away by the flood.
Его́ уби́ло мо́лнией.	He was killed by lightning.

This does *not* mean that an impersonal construction *must* be used to describe an accident. If an accident is caused by a concrete instrument, a straightforward active construction is normal:

Авто́бус задави́л ребёнка.	the child was run over by a bus.

(6) This neuter singular construction may be used even if a human agent is responsible for the action, but only if there is an element of accident in the action. On the other hand the third person plural construction (see (3)) expresses intentional action. It is therefore natural to say

Его́ уби́ли в рукопа́шном бою́	he was killed in hand-to-hand fighting

but

Его́ уби́ло при перестре́лке.	he was killed in the firing.

6. COMPARISON OF ENGLISH PASSIVE STATEMENTS WITH RUSSIAN TRANSLATIONS

The various means of expressing the passive in Russian have now been discussed in some detail. To give a balanced general picture of the subject, however, it is instructive to compare English literary texts with recent Russian translations of them and to note the frequency with which the various constructions are used. A

39

typical example is John Braine's *Room at the Top*, which contains a lot of conversational English as well as 'literary' descriptive passages, and has been translated into Russian by T. Ozerskaya and T. Kudryavtseva. Examples given in this section are taken from this work.

A. *Imperfective aspect*

(1) In 250 pages of text there are a dozen main verbs with inanimate subjects which require an imperfective passive construction in Russian. Half of them are rendered by reflexive verbs:

It was as if the names of rooms were taken quite literally.	Назва́ния ко́мнат в до́ме тёти Э́мили понима́лись, по-ви́домому, соверше́нно буква́льно.
At the time the houses in Oak Crescent were built, it wasn't considered that the working classes needed baths.	В те го́ды, когда́ Дубо́вый Зигза́г то́лько начина́л застра́иваться, счита́лось, что рабо́чим ва́нны ни к чему́.
Towels were kept in the cistern-cupboard.	Полоте́нца храни́лись в бельево́м ба́ке.
...if every business were run as even the most slatternly urban district council, then Americans would come over here to learn the techniques of greater productivity.	е́сли бы ка́ждое предприя́тие управля́лось с тако́й же чёткостью, как са́мый захуда́лый городско́й райо́н, тогда́ америка́нцам пришло́сь бы учи́ться у нас повыше́нию труда́.
...the moors are Gilden's maquis and behind its walls are planned the sudden raid into the valley, the ambush in the village, the last desperate stand with the enemy corpses piling up behind the drystone walls.	ве́ресковые пу́стоши — э́то ги́лденские маки́, а за стена́ми фе́рмы выраба́тываются пла́ны неожи́данного налёта на доли́ну, заса́ды в посёлке и после́днего отча́янного сопротивле́ния, когда́ тру́пы враго́в бу́дут гру́дами нава́лены за кладби́щенской стено́й.
Here was the place where decisions were taken, deals made between soup and sweet...	Это бы́ло ме́сто, где ме́жду су́пом и десе́ртом принима́лись реше́ния и заключа́лись сде́лки...

The other examples are converted into non-passive constructions: e.g.

...it seemed impossible that they should be read.	...тру́дно бы́ло пове́рить, что кто́-то мог их чита́ть.
...with none of those solid merits, for the sake of which so much can be forgiven.	...без тех соли́дных досто́инств, ра́ди кото́рых мно́гое мо́жно прости́ть.

Sometimes an intransitive verb is used, e.g.:

The piano top was bare, a sure sign that it was used as a musical instrument and not as an auxiliary mantlepiece.	На крышке рояля ничего не стояло и не лежало — верный признак того, что рояль здесь служил музыкальным инструментом, а не чем-то вроде каминной полки.

Where the subject is animate, the reflexive passive is used less frequently. Out of twelve main verbs only two are reflexive in Russian:

...the men inside were being fried in their own fat like bacon.	...люди там...запекаются в собственном соку, как окорока.
Whatever desires they had been tormented by, I had fulfilled...	Пока они терзаются несбыточными желаниями, я уже осуществил то, к чему они стремятся...

In the other instances conversion takes place, usually with an active construction:

It was as if I were being attacked by an invisible enemy.	У меня было такое чувство, словно меня преследует какой-то невидимый враг.
I thought I was no longer deceived by the mirage.	Подумал я...мираж уже не обманывает.
I don't mean that I was personally overawed by all the splendid people there...	Не то чтобы меня очень уж подавляли посещавшие это кафе важные особы...
I felt as if I were being sent home...	Я чувствовал себя так, словно меня отсылают домой...

Occasionally an English construction can best be translated into Russian with the help of a new clause, and here too the tendency to avoid the reflexive passive with an animate subject is observed. Here are some examples:

I felt myself being pushed into the position of the poor man at the gate...	Я чувствовал, что мне хотят отвести место жалкого побирушки у чёрного крыльца...
And we don't mind being reminded of him.	Не пугаемся, когда что-нибудь напоминает нам о нём.
I joined the Thespians with the vision of being constantly embraced by handsome young men.	Я пошла к «Служителям Мельпомены» в надежде, что меня будут обнимать красивые молодые люди.

41

(2) Other means of expressing the imperfective passive as the main verb of a clause are extremely rare.

In 250 pages there is not a single example of the construction using быть with the present passive participle (e.g. былá читáема). There is one example of the use of бывáть with the perfective past passive participle:

...at the Technical College, where to some extent they are forced to rub shoulders with the common people...

...в Политехнѝческом институ́те; там бу́дущие ле́ддерсфордские магнáты бывáют вы́нуждены общáться с просты́м лю́дом...

There is also one example of an imperfective past passive participle used in its short form with the verb 'to be' (in this instance 'understood'):

Perhaps, I thought, one was earmarked from birth, and only the scoundrels and the geniuses ever rose out of the class into which they were born.

Вероя́тно, поду́мал я, все мы ме́чены с рожде́ния, и то́лько ге́ниям или негодя́ям удаётся вы́рваться за ра́мки своего́ кла́сса.

(3) The present passive participle used attributively occurs on average about every thirty pages, which seems to be normal. Here are two examples:

As long as I kept on walking they (i.e. memories) would remain mixed and chaotic, like imperfectly recollected books and films.

Пока́ я продолжа́л шага́ть, э́то бы́ли спу́танные, беспоря́дочные виде́ния, подо́бные сму́тно припоминáемым отры́вкам из фѝльмов и книг.

...the river was running faster than usual, swollen with melted snow and harried by the north-east wind.

...Вздýвшаяся от растáявшего снéга, подстёгиваемая сéверовосто́чным вéтром рекá быстрéй обы́чного катѝла свой во́ды.

The reflexive participle is used twice with passive meaning, although there is no corresponding participle in the English:

Alice gave me a light little smile (translated as 'over Alice's lips there passed a fleeting smile intended for me').

По губáм Э́лис скольвну́ла мимолётная улы́бка, предназначáвшаяся для меня́.

It's only for four days we shan't be getting our money's worth (translated as 'It is only for four days that we shall not be enjoying the benefits due to us).

Мы всего́ четы́ре дня не бýдем пóльзоваться причитáющимися нам блáгами.

(4) The imperfective past passive participle used as an attribute is rarer, occurring only once every sixty pages on average, and even in these few examples most of the participles could be regarded as adjectives. In the following quotations мощённые is a participle, whereas мятый and битое are adjectivalized:

the narrow cobbled streets...	у́зкие, мощённые булы́жником у́лочки...
...the coat was badly wrinkled and smelled of rubber.	...плащ воня́л рези́ной и был како́й-то мя́тый.
There was no rubble now, no broken glass.	Би́тое стекло́, ще́бень бы́ли давно́ у́браны.

в. *Perfective aspect*

(1) Instances of the use of the perfective passive formed with быть and the short form of the past passive participle are too numerous to be worth counting: there are five on the first two pages. These constructions mostly have inanimate subjects:

The other evening I found a photo of myself taken shortly after I came to live at Warley. My hair is plastered into a skullcap, my collar doesn't fit, and the knot of my tie, held in place by a hideous pin, shaped like a dagger, is far too small.	На дня́х мне попа́лся в ру́ки сни́мок, сде́ланный вско́ре по́сле моего́ прие́зда в Уо́рли. Во́лосы прили́заны донельзя́, воротничо́к сиди́т пло́хо, у́зел га́лстука завя́зан сли́шком ту́го и уде́рживается на ме́сте чудо́вищной була́вкой в фо́рме кинжа́ла.

It is interesting to note that frequently a perfective passive participle is used where none occurs in English. There is an example of this in the above quotation. Of course, the subject of this construction is often animate:

I'm forced to be a living proof of the firm's prosperity.	Я вы́нужден служи́ть живы́м доказа́тельсвом процвета́ния на́шей фи́рмы.
At first we used to number them.	Понача́лу все они́ у нас бы́ли перенумеро́ваны.
But Alice had been killed.	Но Элис была́ уби́та.
The first dragon was killed, even if it only was a small one.	Пе́рвый драко́н — пусть совсе́м тщеду́шный — был сражён напова́л.
...The Glittering Zombie, a simple soul whose father had been a Corpo-	...Сверка́ющий Зо́мби — проста́я душа́ (его́ оте́ц до войны́ был

43

ration dustman before the war, was, as always, impressed and flattered.

городски́м му́сорщиком), — как всегда́ в таки́х слу́чаях, был не́сколько пода́влен и польщён.

(2) The tendency to convert a passive to an active statement is stronger with an animate subject: out of twenty main verbs (with animate subjects) which are passive in English and require a perfective verb in Russian, thirteen are 'converted'.

I was overcome by depression.	мно́ю овладе́ло уны́ние.
I was a little surprised that Mrs Thompson should so prominently display the picture of her dead son.	Меня́ слегка́ удиви́ло, что ми́ссис То́мпсон пове́сила фотогра́фию своего́ поко́йного сы́на на столь ви́дном ме́сте.
I was astounded and delighted by her naivety.	её на́ивность изуми́ла меня́ и привела́ в восто́рг.
I was aware that she was in control of the conversation, that Bob had been steered away from some dangerous corner.	я почу́вствовал, что ми́ссис То́мпсон уме́ло руководи́ла бесе́дой и помеша́ла Бо́бу косну́ться како́й-то опа́сной те́мы.

A good proportion of these conversions are made with the third person plural construction:

His manner indicated the subject was closed and I'd been put in my place.	Тон Джо́рджа пока́зывал, что те́ма исче́рпана и меня́ поста́вили на ме́сто.

(Note the participle with the inanimate subject те́ма and the switch to the third person plural active construction for the animate.)

(she) had been taken to hospital in the middle of the night.	среди́ но́чи её увезли́ в больни́цу.
It's like bribing an executioner; if you're reprieved, he says it's due to his efforts and if you're hanged, you can't talk.	Это вро́де взя́тки палачу́. Если вас поми́луют, он ска́жет, что э́то произошло́ благодаря́ его́ стара́ниям, а е́сли вас пове́сят, вам уже́ ничего́ не уда́стся сказа́ть.
There was only one male St Clair left and he was killed in the 1914 war.	А после́днего Сент-Кле́ра уби́ли на войне́ четы́рнадцатого го́да.

This may be compared with the following sentence, where the person killed was killed by accident:

Your grandma had all t'heart knocked out of her when your grandpa wor killed at t'mill.	Когда́ твоего́ де́душку уби́ло на заво́де, ба́бушка совсе́м па́ла ду́хом.

There is clearly a tendency to use an active statement rather than a passive if the subject of the English sentence is animate and the action is performed by a person or persons known or unknown. Conversion of this kind does make it clear that the statement is concerned with an action, whereas the past participle could emphasize a state.

(3) The use of a perfective reflexive verb to translate a passive construction is inevitably rare. There are some half dozen such verbs in the text but they mostly occur where the translation is somewhat free.

...and the atmosphere of flirtatiousness and self-aware femininity...was instantly dispelled.

...и атмосфе́ра вла́стно пробужда́вшейся же́нственности и полуде́тского коке́тства...мгнове́нно развея́лась.

...the imitation oak panelling was pulped with dust and smoke and weather.

...а пане́ли разбу́хли под де́йствием дождя́, пропита́лись гря́вью и са́жей.

Now the original village with its grey stone houses clustered round the cobbled market square has been surrounded by a sort of dermoid cyst of pebbledash and brick and concrete. But the woods are still there...

Тепе́рь же вокру́г стари́нных до́миков из се́рого ка́мня, сгруди́вшихся у мощёной булы́жником ры́ночной пло́щади, образова́лся уро́дливый наро́ст из штукату́рки, кирпича́ и бето́на. Но ро́ща сохрани́лась...

7. CONCLUSIONS

It is not really possible to establish definitive rules for the expression of the passive in Russian. In many cases more than one construction is possible, although there may be differences of emphasis in the various constructions. These differences have been pointed out in the course of the foregoing discussion, but in conclusion the main points may be summed up as follows:

(1) Where an imperfective construction is required the reflexive verb is commonly used for inanimate subjects, but care must be taken if the subject is animate: 'conversion' will probably be most convenient.

(2) The present passive participle with быть is used to emphasize the idea of the passive action, the process itself, but this is a rare construction.

(3) The imperfective past passive participle with быть is also a rare construction and is usually used for colloquial or archaic effect.

(4) The perfective past passive participle with быть tends to denote a state, the result of an action rather than the action itself, and if there is a need to stress the action, 'conversion' may be necessary; in comparatively rare cases a perfective reflexive verb will be suitable.

8. BIBLIOGRAPHY

BARKHUDAROV, S. G. (ed.). *Словарь русского языка*, 4 тт. Государственное издательство иностранных и национальных словарей, Moscow, 1957–61.

CHERNYSHOV, V. I. (ed.). *Словарь современного русского литературного языка*. Академия наук, Moscow-Leningrad, 1950–.

FILIN, F. P. 'О двух значениях глаголов, образованных посредством префикса на- и суффикса -ся', *Вопросы грамматики, сборник в честь...И. И. Мещанинова*. Академия наук, Moscow-Leningrad, 1960.

GALKINA-FEDORUK, E. M. (ed.). *Современный русский язык, ч. 2: морфология, синтаксис*. Издательство Московского универститета, Moscow, 1964.

GVOZDEV, A. N. *Очерки по стилистике русского языка*. Академия педагогических наук, Moscow, 1952.

LOMTEV, T. P. *Основы синтаксиса современного русского языка*. Учпедгиз, Moscow, 1958.

OZHEGOV, S. I. *Словарь русского языка* (изд. 5). Государственное издательство иностранных и национальных словарей, Moscow, 1956.

PESHKOVSKY, A. M. *Русский синтаксис в научном освещении* (изд. 7). Учпедгиз, Moscow, 1956.

POTEBNYA, A. A. *Из записок по русской грамматике, 4: глагол, местоимение, числительное, предлог*. Академия наук, Moscow-Leningrad, 1941.

PUL'KINA, I. M. & ZAKHAVA-NEKRASOVA, E. V. *Учебник русского языка для студентов-иностранцев*. Высшая школа, Moscow, 1952.

SHAKHMATOV, A. A. *Из трудов по современному русскому языку*, Moscow, 1952.

USHAKOV, D. N. (ed.). *Толковый словарь русского языка*, 4 тт. Огиз, Moscow, 1935–40.

VALGINA, N. S., *et al. Современный русский язык* (изд. 2). Высшая школа, Moscow, 1964.

VINOGRADOV, V. V. (ed.). *Грамматика русского языка*, 3 тт. Академия наук, Moscow-Leningrad, 1952–4.

VINOGRADOV, V. V. *Русский язык*. Учпедгиз, Moscow, 1947.

BORRAS, F. M. & CHRISTIAN, R. F. *Russian Syntax*. Oxford University Press, 1959.

MORISON, W. A. *Studies in Russian Forms and Uses—the present gerund and active participle*. Faber, London, 1959.

MORISON, W. A. 'Logical stress and grammatical form in Russian', *Slavonic and East European Review*, XLII, 292–311. London, 1964.

SEMEONOFF, A. H. *Russian Syntax*. Dent, London, 1962.

UNBEGAUN, B. O. *Russian Grammar*. Oxford University Press, 1959.

WARD, D. *The Russian Language Today*. Hutchinson, London, 1965.

AGREEMENT OF THE VERB-PREDICATE
WITH A COLLECTIVE SUBJECT

by J. MULLEN

Contemporary Soviet usage, both in the press and in literary works, shows some apparent inconsistency in the choice of a singular or plural verb-predicate where the action of the verb is ascribed either to a singular collective noun (большинствó, ряд, etc.) or to such words as нéсколько, скóлько, мнóго, мáло. This is recognized by Vinogradov, who writes (475) that in cases where a plural verb is made to agree with a singular collective noun 'the plural form of the verb, as if independently of the form of the "subject", directly denotes the number of agents. It refers directly to the concrete action and its performers. It agrees with the lexical meaning of the "subject". No agreement, however, takes place with the form of the noun that expresses the subject of the action.'

As Rozental' points out (1960: 8), the correct literary form of agreement has traditionally been considered to be the grammatical one, i.e. a singular collective subject requires a singular verb. Bulakhovsky remarks (244) that 'with скóлько, мнóго the singular is obligatory'. The Academy Grammar (507) contains a similar statement: 'The use of a plural predicate with a subject that includes the words мáло, мнóго has a colloquial effect.' Galkina-Fedoruk (182), while admitting that some collective subjects may take a verb-predicate in the plural, says that if the subject consists of a noun with quantitative meaning combined with a genitive case, then the predicate agrees with the subject in gender and number. She quotes the following examples:

Стой, стой, — кричáла мáсса голосóв. (Prishvin, Берендéева рóща)	'Stop, stop!' they all shouted at once.
И вот цéлая *лавúна* кáменьев, глыб и кóмьев землú *рýшится* в прóпасть с нарастáющим устремлéнием... (Fedin, Пéрвые рáдости)	And now a whole avalanche of stones, boulders and lumps of earth poured down into the abyss with increasing momentum.

Among Soviet writers who admit that a plural agreement may be used in the literary language, Galkina-Fedoruk (182) gives no detailed account of the possible reasons affecting the choice of singular or plural agreement. She merely notes the fact that with несколько, сколько, столько, мало, много, большинство, the predicate is normally singular, but that cases occur where such words have a verb-predicate in the plural. She adds that the predicate is usually plural with a subject denoting animate beings. Gvozdev (68) says that singular agreement is the literary norm, but that the plural may be used, especially when persons are named. He quotes the example:

Бóльшая часть выступáвших не соглаcúлись с доклáдчиком.	Most of those who spoke did not agree with the rapporteur.

The question is discussed in some detail by Rozental' (1957: 99–101; 1960: 1–11), who lists a number of factors affecting the choice of agreement. He writes that plural agreement is usual when one or more of the following conditions exist:

(*a*) the predicate is at some distance from the subject;

(*b*) the collective noun is followed by several dependent words in the genitive plural (большинство писáтелей, поэ́тов, крúтиков...);

(*c*) the sentence contains more than one predicate dependent on the subject;

(*d*) the action of the persons expressed by the subject-group is emphasized;

(*e*) the idea of a plurality of performers of the action is emphasized by the use of a participial construction or a relative clause with котóрый, the participle or the word котóрый being plural (большинство лиц, выступáвших в прéниях...; ряд студéнтов, котóрые успéшно защитúли диплóмный проéкт...).

Rozental' adds that, whether or not the conditions outlined above exist in a given sentence, there has recently become noticeable a tendency in the press and in colloquial speech to prefer plural agreement, whereas the strictly 'correct' grammatical agreement, i.e. the use of a singular predicate, still predominates in literary works. However, the present survey of 320 examples taken from contemporary literary works and from Soviet newspapers and periodicals suggests different conclusions.

The question whether to use singular or plural agreement does not normally arise when a collective noun-subject *stands on its own*, i.e. has no quantitative meaning and is not followed by a noun in the genitive or a pronoun governed by из. In such cases, both in literature and in the press, singular agreement is customary, e.g.

Собралáсь вся молодёжь.	All the young people had come.
Крестьянство боролось прóтив помéщиков.	The peasantry fought against their landlords.

Exceptions to this rule are found only in special circumstances, as in the example quoted by Rozental' from L. Tolstoy:

Всё *дворянство возненавидело* меня всéми сйлами душй и *суют* мне пáлки в колёса со всех сторóн.	The whole of the gentry have taken the strongest dislike to me and are putting spokes in my wheels from every side.

Here the use of a plural verb-predicate in the second part of the sentence is possibly determined by the distance of the predicate from the subject and by the author's wish to emphasize the plurality of performers of the action.

Where the subject of the sentence is a noun with quantitative meaning, three types of construction occur:

(*a*) the collective noun has *no noun or pronoun* dependent on it;

(*b*) the collective noun governs a noun or pronoun in the *genitive singular*;

(*c*) the collective noun governs a noun or pronoun in the *genitive plural*.

In the first two cases the verb-predicate is normally singular, for the absence of a dependent plural noun or pronoun weakens the idea of plurality that would otherwise be present in the mind of the writer:

Вйдно, *большинствó ужé удовлетворило* свой разýмные потрéбности в цйтрусовых. (V. Aksyonov, Апельсйны из Марóкко)	Evidently the majority had already satisfied their reasonable requirements for citrus fruit.
А у нас *большинствó* молодёжи о войнé смýтно *пóмнит.* (A. Chakovsky, Свет далёкой ввезды)	But most of our young people have only a dim recollection of the war.
Бóльшая часть насéления Латйнской Амéрики (ва исключéнием Бразйлии) *говорйт* на испáнском языкé. (Наýка и Жизнь, no. 11, 1964)	The greater part of the population of Latin America (excluding Brazil) speak Spanish.

Occasional exceptions to this rule occur, but usually in contexts where special conditions exist which would make a singular

4   нео

predicate seem unnatural. Rozental' quotes the following examples:

Большинство́ серьёзно, да́же мра́чно *смотре́ли* на э́ту живу́ю карти́ну тяжёлого безысхо́дного разду́мья и со вздо́хом *отходи́ли.* (L. Andreyev)	The majority looked gravely, even gloomily at this living picture of depressed and hopeless meditation and moved away with a sigh.
Преоблада́ла молодёжь. Лишь *меньшинство́ бы́ли* людьми́ пожилы́ми, умудрёнными о́пытом.	Young people predominated. Only a minority were elderly people, made wise by experience.

In the first example the second verb-predicate отходи́ли denotes a series of actions performed by different individuals, so that the sense requires the use of a plural, while the first verb-predicate смотре́ли is made plural in order that it should not clash with the second. In the other example the verb is influenced by its plural predicate людьми́ пожилы́ми, so that there occurs a kind of inverted agreement which avoids the inconvenience of the combination бы́ло людьми́.

Similarly, special contextual circumstances influence the choice of agreement in the following sentence:

В за́ле бы́ло мно́го делега́тов: *большинство́* уже́ *за́няли* предоста́вленные им места́.	There were many delegates in the hall: most had already occupied the seats allocated to them.

In this sentence it is the pronoun им that makes it necessary to use a plural verb-predicate. It would be inappropriate to say *Большинство́* уже́ *за́няло* предоста́вленные им места́, using a singular verb and plural pronoun to refer to the same people; but it would be equally inappropriate to say *Большинство́* уже́ *за́няло* предоста́вленные ему́ места́, since the seats are thought of as having been allocated to individual members of the group, not to the group as a whole.

In the third type of sentence, where the collective noun has quantitative meaning and governs a noun or pronoun in the *genitive plural*, the question whether to use a singular or plural verb-predicate is more complex. The choice of agreement depends partly on the conditions of the context, partly on the preference of the individual writer. Rozental' states (1960: 6) that 'although in the language of literary works grammatical agreement—with the predicate in the singular—predominates, in the style used by publicists there has recently become noticeable a tendency to prefer agreement according to sense, with a predicate in the plural'. Among other examples he quotes:

Ещё недáвно *большинствó* предстáвленных на конферéнции стран *бы́ли* бесправными колóниями.
(Прáвда, 3 January 1958)

Until quite recently the majority of the countries represented at the conference were colonies deprived of their rights.

Часть егó интúмных друзéй *шлют* емý привéты из тюрьмы́, где отбывáют наказáние.
(Литератýрная газéта, 13 June 1957)

Some of his intimate friends send him greetings from the prison where they are serving their sentence.

Ряд конкрéтных вопрóсов, котóрые возникáют как в связú с предложéнием Совéтского Сою́за, так и в связú с предложéнием Соединённых Штáтов, ещё нé *были* подвéргнуты дóлжному рассмотрéнию.
(Прáвда, 26 September 1954)

A number of concrete questions arising both from the Soviet and from the United States' proposals had still not been given due consideration.

However, two of these three sentences cannot be regarded as typical, for they illustrate types of context that favour the choice of a plural predicate. The first one is an example of the inverted agreement already noted, where a plural verb is used in order to avoid a clash with a plural noun-predicate (бы́ло бесправными колóниями). The third sentence contains a lengthy relative clause introduced by котóрые and separating the verb-predicate нé были подвéргнуты from its subject ряд; this also is a type of construction which, as Rozental' himself points out, emphasizes the idea of plurality and causes most writers to prefer a plural verb-predicate.

In general there is little difference between the various types of collective subject—большинствó, мнóго, бóльшая часть, etc.—in the frequency with which they take a singular or plural verb-predicate. Normally it is the construction of the sentence that determines the choice of agreement. An exception to this rule is ряд, which is almost invariably used with a singular predicate even in contexts where other collective subjects normally have a plural verb. The following example illustrates the point:

Ряд вúдных представúтелей совéтской общéственности, в числé котóрых председáтель Совéтского комитéта солидáрности стран Áзии

A number of leading representatives of Soviet public opinion, including Mirzo Tursunzade, Chairman of the Soviet Committee of Solidarity with

4-2

и Африки, лауреат Ленинской премии Мирзо Турсун-заде, член-корреспондент АН СССР, заместитель председателя Советского комитета солидарности стран Азии и Африки Б. Г. Гафуров, академик, член президиума Советского комитета солидарности стран Азии и Африки Е. М. Жуков, председатель Советского комитета защиты мира Н. С. Тихонов, *выступил* с протестом в связи с процессом в Лоренсу-Маркише.

(Правда, 19 March 1966)

the countries of Asia and Africa and Lenin prize-winner, B. G. Gafurov, Corresponding Member of the USSR Academy of Sciences and Deputy-Chairman of the Soviet Committee of Solidarity with the countries of Asia and Africa, E. M. Zhukov, Academician and Member of the Praesidium of the Soviet Committee of Solidarity with the countries of Asia and Africa, and N. S. Tikhonov, Chairman of the Soviet Committee for the Defence of Peace, protested against the trial in Lourenço Marques.

As will be seen below, where the question is discussed in more detail, this type of sentence, in which the predicate is separated from the subject by a lengthy intervening section of text, is one that favours the choice of a plural verb. That a singular verb is nevertheless used in the example quoted above, where the idea of plurality is reinforced by an unusually long intervening text listing a number of names and titles, suggests that either the author or the proof-reader feels a plural predicate to be inadmissible with ряд in any circumstances.

Among the various types of construction affecting the choice of agreement, great consistency is shown by Soviet writers in the use of a singular predicate where the main verb in the sentence is *passive*. In the present survey sixty-seven out of seventy-one of the examples of this type of sentence have singular agreement. The following are typical:

Большинство из них и без этого *было связано* с «Современником» давними узами и *печаталось* почти исключительно в нём.
(К. I. Chukovsky, Люди и книги)

Most of them, apart from this, had long since been linked with 'The Contemporary' and had their work printed almost exclusively in it.

О высоком уровне подготовки войск свидетельствуют результаты воздушных и ракетных стрельб в истёкшем году, подавляющее *большинство* которых *выполнено* с высокими оценками.
(Советская Россия, 19 April 1966)

The high level of the forces' training is borne out by the results of the air and rocket firing exercises in the past year, in the overwhelming majority of which high marks were scored.

The few exceptions to this rule that occur can usually be explained by the presence of special circumstances that would make a singular predicate inappropriate, as in this example:

И если б у нас *были освоены* несколько таких мест — в Хибинах, Карпатах, на Урале, — зимние отпуска явно стали бы более популярны.
(Неделя, 12 March 1966)

And if we had in use several such places—in the Khibin mountains, the Carpathians, the Urals—winter holidays would clearly become more popular.

Here the verb is plural because it is closely followed by a list of specific nouns subsumed by несколько; attention is thus drawn to the individuality, the plurality, of the places mentioned, with the effect that the collective sense of несколько is weakened.

Singular agreement is consistently used not only in sentences where the verb is passive, but also where a verb that is grammatically active denotes a *state* rather than an action. All forty-four verbs of this type (быть, стоять, существовать, представлять собой, иметься, etc.) occurring in the present survey were used in the singular:

Было у меня в лаборатории *немало* хороших людей и специалистов замечательных.
(A. Chakovsky, Свет далёкой звезды)

In my laboratory I had quite a few good people and outstanding specialists.

Хотя современная индонезийская армия сложилась в ходе боёв против японских оккупантов и голландских колонизаторов, в её офицерском составе *имёлось* и *имеется немало* представителей компрадорско-феодальных кругов.
(Известия, 14 March 1966)

Although the modern Indonesian Army was formed in the course of the battles against the Japanese occupation forces and the Dutch colonialists, its officer corps has always contained a number of representatives of feudal compradore circles.

The converse of the rule that the predicate is usually singular with a passive verb or with an active verb that denotes a state is that a plural predicate is preferred with a verb or in a construction that emphasizes the *activity* of the persons comprising the subject of the sentence. One type of sentence that produces such an emphasis is that in which the collective subject is followed by more than one genitive plural noun denoting persons; this type of construction puts the emphasis on the people mentioned and on their actions rather than on the singular collective noun forming the subject, so that the verb is made to agree by sense:

Между тем *большинство* рецензёнтов и критиков даже не *приметили* Ивана Степаныча.
(K. I. Chukovsky, Люди и книги)

Meanwhile the majority of reviewers and critics did not even notice Ivan Stepanych.

A similar effect is produced by the use of *more than one verb-predicate* dependent on the collective subject; the repetition of verbs at some distance from each other draws attention to the actions carried out by the subject, while the separation at least of the second and any subsequent predicates from the subject weakens the sense of grammatical dependence on the collective noun. This leads to the use of a verb that agrees with the plural sense of the subject:

Большинствó учёных *перечúты-вали* рабóты по теóрии относúтель-ности и *смотрéли* в потолкú свóих кабинéтов.
(Наýка и Жизнь, no. 9, 1964)

Most of the scientists were rereading works on the theory of relativity and staring at the ceiling in their rooms.

A third type of sentence occurs in which the collective sense of such subjects as нéсколько, большинствó, etc., is weakened: this is the type in which the verb-predicate used calls attention to the *independent activity* of the persons forming part of the subject-group. An example of such a verb is разойтúсь, which necessarily denotes the separate actions of the individuals in the subject-group and therefore requires a plural verb:

Бóльшая часть студéнтов ужé *разошлúсь.*

Most of the students had already gone their separate ways.

With other verbs that do not in themselves suggest independent action by the members of the subject-group the context may nevertheless indicate that separate actions are being carried out, as in these examples:

К концý рабóчего дня, когдá *большинствó* егó коллéг обы́чно ужé *уходúли* из управлéния, он позвонúл Дженнингсу.
(Наýка и Жизнь, no. 9, 1964)

Towards the end of the working day, when usually most of his colleagues had already left the head office, he rang Jennings.

Не удивúтельно, что так *мнóго* худóжников *дéлали* егó портрéты.
(Недéля, 26 March 1966)

It is not surprising that so many artists have done portraits of him.

Одновремéнно с э́тим *мнóго* другúх америкáнских самолётов *бомбúли* и *обстрéливали* гóрод Фулú и густонаселённый райóн в провúн-ции Хайзыóнг, — сообщáет агéнт-ство ВИА.
(Совéтская Россúя, 19 April 1966)

At the same time many other American aeroplanes bombed and strafed the town of Fuli and a heavily populated area in the province of Khaizyong, reports the Vietnamese News Agency.

The grammatical singularity of a collective subject tends to be disregarded when the subject-group is separated from its predicate by a *lengthy intervening passage of text*. This may happen when the subject-group is followed by a participial phrase or a relative clause dependent on который; it also happens when the subject-group is expanded by a part of the sentence specifying or describing its members. These examples are typical:

Ско́лько ребя́т, на кото́рых уже́ все махну́ли руко́й, *вы́шли* благодаря́ ему́ на пра́вильный путь!
(Изве́стия, 28 January 1966)

How many lads whom everyone else had given up hope for found the right road thanks to him!

На́дя отверну́лась от Лю́си и ста́ла смотре́ть, как *не́сколько малыше́й*, то́лстых и неуклю́жих в тёплых оде́ждах, *вози́лись* в песке́ на де́тской площа́дке.
(F. Koluntsev, У Ники́тских воро́т)

Nadya turned away from Lyusya and began to watch several small children, fat and clumsy in their warm clothes, playing in the sand in the playground.

Regardless of other contextual considerations, a plural verb is normally used when the subject-group has dependent on it not only a verb but also an adjective in the short form. This reflects the unwillingness of writers either to use a different number for a verb and an adjective dependent on the same subject, or to use a singular adjective with a collective subject. The following example shows none of the features that normally favour a plural verb-predicate, so that the choice of a plural verb may be assumed to be due to the presence of a following adjective also dependent on the subject-group:

Сейча́с *большинство́* рабо́тающих *пита́ются* в столо́вых и о́чень *дово́льны* э́тим.
(Пра́вда, 2 April 1966)

Now the majority of the employees eat in canteens and are very satisfied with this.

One other case occurs in which a plural predicate tends to be used, although not with such consistency as in the cases mentioned above: this is the type of sentence in which the subject consists of an approximation. Here too the use of a singular verb-predicate has traditionally been considered the literary norm. The Academy Grammar (503) states: 'The predicate is used in the singular with a subject denoting an approximate quantity. The sense of approximation may be expressed either lexically by means of an adverb (свы́ше, о́коло, ме́нее, ме́ньше, бо́лее, бо́льше), or by the use of the preposition с with the numeral, or by the word-

55

order, e.g.: В классе *сидело не меньше двадцати* человек ("There were at least twenty people in the class"); *Пришло человек с пятьдесят* ("About fifty people came"); У ворот *стояло человек пять* ("About five people were standing at the gates").' The Grammar then goes on to quote a series of examples of approximation in which a singular verb is used, most of which are, however, taken from classical authors of the nineteenth century. Rozental' on the other hand states (1960: 10) that 'at the present time there is a marked preponderance in this case of agreement according to sense, i.e. the use of a predicate in the plural, independently of the way in which the category of approximation is expressed—lexically (by means of the words более, менее, свыше, около, etc.) or grammatically (by the word-order—postposition of the numeral)'. He quotes examples taken exclusively from the press in which a plural predicate is used with approximations not only in constructions which would normally favour a plural verb, but also in constructions where the singular is normally used, e.g. where subject and verb are inverted, with a passive verb, or with an inanimate subject:

Приступили к занятиям *более 1700* студентов Московского вечёрнего машиностройтельного института.
(Вечёрняя Москва, 10 February 1954)

More than 1700 students of the Moscow Evening Engineering Institute have started on their studies.

Как сообщает американская печать из Порт-о-Прéнса (Гайти)... *около тысячи* человек *были загнаны* штыками в грузовики и *увезены* в тюрьмы.
(Правда, 19 June 1957)

As the American press reports from Port-au-Prince (Haiti)...about a thousand people were driven at bayonet-point into lorries and taken off to prison.

Свыше 70 театров страны *покажут* в эти дни чéховские спектакли.
(Литератýрная газéта, 24 June 1954)

More than 70 of the country's theatres will be performing plays by Chekhov at this time.

However, the preference for a plural predicate with an approximation is not so marked as Rozental', who quotes a long series of exclusively plural examples, would seem to suggest. Among the examples collected for the present survey, singular predicates predominate (twenty-three out of thirty), while Rozental's examples of plural verbs used in normally unfavourable circum-

56

stances can be paralleled by examples where singular verbs are used in contexts that would normally favour a plural. This example, typical of many to be found in the press, illustrates the use of a singular verb with an approximation in which the subject-group incorporates animate beings:

Тепéрь онó организóвано по óтраслям произвóдства, в нём *учáствует свы́ше 90 процéнтов* рабóчих и слýжащих.
(Прáвда, 2 April 1966)

Now it [socialist competition] is organized in the various branches of production, and more than 90 per cent of workers and other employees take part in it.

Among constructions in which a singular verb-predicate is most consistently used is the type in which the subject-group denotes a unified whole. The overwhelming majority of the examples collected for the present survey (sixty-seven out of sixty-eight) have singular agreement in this type of context, even when the construction is otherwise such as would lead one to expect a plural verb. The subject-group is regarded as an indivisible whole when the following conditions exist:

(1) The subject consists of an expression of time, e.g.

Лагунов никогдá не летáл, и бог знáет *скóлько лет прошлó* с тех пор, как Лагунов рабóтал с прибóрами.
(D. Granin, Идý на грозý)

Lagunov had never flown, and God knows how many years had gone by since he had worked with instruments.

Прошлó ещё *нéсколько* днéй, и Лизе стáло я́сно, что онá ошиблась.
(A. Chakovsky, Свет далёкой звезды́)

A few more days went by, and Liza realized that she had made a mistake.

(2) The subject is a spatial expression or an approximate measurement, e.g.

...до тогó дóма, где помещáлся райкóм комсомóла, *оставáлось* буквáльно *нéсколько* шагóв.
(G. Gor, Университéтская нáбережная)

There literally remained only a few steps to...the house where the district committee of the Komsomol was quartered.

На их сооружéние *ушлó нéсколько* деся́тков вагóнов ги́пса.
(Литератýрная газéта, 10 March 1966)

Several dozen wagonloads of plaster were used in their construction.

(3) The subject is a homogeneous group such as the population of a city or the crowd at a meeting, e.g.

На у́лицах бы́ло не осо́бенно лю́дно, *большинство́* мурманча́н всё же *спа́ло* ми́рным сном, сообразу́ясь с часа́ми, а не с со́лнцем.
(V. Voevodin, Бу́йная голову́шка)

There were not many people on the streets; most of the inhabitants of Murmansk were sleeping peacefully, taking their cue from the clock and not from the sun.

В большо́м за́ле *собрало́сь мно́го* люде́й. (Неде́ля, 16 April 1966)

A lot of people had collected in the large hall.

The tendency towards singular agreement in the type of sentence where the members of the subject-group are regarded as a single unit is so strong that other considerations favouring a plural predicate, such as the presence of a noun-predicate in the plural, may be disregarded, as in this example:

Носи́телями я́дерного ору́жия *явля́ется* та́кже *бо́льшая часть* истреби́телей-бомбардиро́вщиков такти́ческой и штурмовико́в па́лубной авиа́ции и разли́чные войсковы́е раке́ты.
(Сове́тская Росси́я, 19 April 1966)

Nuclear weapons are also carried by the greater part of the fighter-bombers in the tactical air force and carrier-borne strike aircraft, as well as by various military rockets.

While firm rules cannot be laid down for the form of agreement used with collective subjects, it is possible to indicate the factors which favour the choice of one or the other agreement. These may be summarized as follows:

(1) Singular agreement is preferred when:
    (*a*) the verb-predicate is passive;
    (*b*) the verb used denotes a state rather than an action (быть, существова́ть, etc.);
    (*c*) the collective subject has no noun dependent on it;
    (*d*) the collective subject governs a noun in the genitive singular;
    (*e*) the subject-group appears as a unit;
    (*f*) the subject of the sentence is ряд.

(2) Plural agreement is preferred when
    (*a*) the collective subject and the verb-predicate are widely separated;
    (*b*) the collective subject has dependent on it more than one noun in the genitive plural;

(c) the collective subject governs more than one verb-predicate;

(d) the activity of the persons forming part of the subject-group is emphasized;

(e) the verb has dependent on it a noun-predicate in the plural.

Of the examples used in the present survey, some 90 per cent have their verb in the singular. There is noticeable a marked preference for singular agreement, which has the effect that a singular predicate is often used in contexts where one would normally expect a plural, while the converse occurs much more rarely. The preference for singular agreement, contrary to what Rozental' implies (1960: 6), is particularly marked in the case of examples taken from the press, where it may be that the influence of elementary guides, published for the benefit of proof-readers and stating without qualification that words such as большинство require a singular verb-predicate, leads to the elimination of variation among individual authors. Rozental's view that the authors of literary works are more conservative in this respect is not supported by a study of the material forming the basis of the present survey.

BIBLIOGRAPHY

BULAKHOVSKY, L. A. *Курс русского литературного языка.* Kiev, 1949.

GALKINA-FEDORUK, E. M. (ed.). *Современный русский язык — синтаксис.* МГУ, Moscow, 1957.

Грамматика русского языка, vol. 2. АН СССР, Moscow, 1960.

GVOZDEV, A. N. *Современный русский литературный язык,* vol. 2. Учпедгиз, Moscow, 1958.

MAMONOV, V. A. & ROZENTAL', D. E. *Практическая стилистика современного русского языка.* Искусство, Moscow, 1957.

ROZENTAL', D. E. *Согласование по смыслу сказуемого с подлежащим.* МЗПИ, Moscow, 1960.

VINOGRADOV, V. V. *Русский язык.* Учпедгиз, Moscow, 1947.

For EU product safety concerns, contact us at Calle de José Abascal, 56–1°,
28003 Madrid, Spain or eugpsr@cambridge.org.

www.ingramcontent.com/pod-product-compliance
Ingram Content Group UK Ltd.
Pitfield, Milton Keynes, MK11 3LW, UK
UKHW040616240426
470322UK00010B/148